# ELLIOTT WAVE FIBONACCI HIGH PROBABILITY TRADING

Master The Wave Principle and Market Timing With Proven Strategies

JARROD SANDERS

**Copyright © 2022 Jarrod Sanders - All rights reserved.**

## Legal Notice

This book or parts thereof may not be reproduced in any form, stored in any retrieval system, or transmitted in any form by any means—electronic, mechanical, photocopy, recording, or otherwise—without prior written permission of the publisher, except as provided by United States of America copyright law and fair use.

## Disclaimer Notice

The publisher and the author do not make any guarantee or other promise as to any results that may be obtained from using the content of this book. You should never make any investment decision without first consulting with your own financial advisor and conducting your own research and due diligence. To the maximum extent permitted by law, the publisher and the author disclaim any and all liability in the event any information, commentary, analysis, opinions, advice and/or recommendations contained in this book prove to be inaccurate, incomplete or unreliable, or result in any investment or other losses.

Although the publisher and the author have made every effort to ensure that the information in this book was correct at press time and while this publication is designed to provide accurate information in regard to the subject matter covered, the publisher and the author assume no responsibility for errors, inaccuracies, omissions, or any other inconsistencies herein and hereby disclaim any liability to any party for any loss, damage, or disruption caused by errors or omissions, whether such errors or omissions result from negligence, accident, or any other cause.

# TABLE OF CONTENTS

INTRODUCTION 4

CHAPTER 1: ELLIOTT WAVE FOUNDATIONS 6

CHAPTER 2: MOTIVE WAVES 15

CHAPTER 3: CORRECTIVE WAVES 35

CHAPTER 4: ELLIOTT WAVE GUIDELINES & CHANNELING TECHNIQUES 62

CHAPTER 5: FIBONACCI FOUNDATIONS 76

CHAPTER 6: FIBONACCI AND THE IMPULSE PHASE 87

CHAPTER 7: FIBONACCI AND THE CORRECTIVE PHASE 101

CHAPTER 8: TRADING STRATEGY NO.1 109

CHAPTER 9: TRADING STRATEGY NO.2 131

CHAPTER 10: TRADING STRATEGY NO.3 147

CHAPTER 11: TRADING STRATEGY NO.4 163

CHAPTER 12: TRADING STRATEGY NO.5 176

CONCLUSION 189

REFERENCES 191

# INTRODUCTION

The Elliott Wave principle and Fibonacci tools have become quite popular among technical traders of different trading styles, however, the sad news is that most traders are still struggling with how to make the best use of them to generate consistent profits.

One of the most challenging tasks for Elliott Wave and Fibonacci students is how to combine them to build a cohesive trading strategy. More often than not, the way traders combine the tools is at the elementary level only, and cannot unleash the full power within them that can otherwise be achieved when we look at them from some different aspects.

In this book, I'm going to reveal everything you'll need to know about using Elliott Wave and Fibonacci tools effectively and profitably. Instead of relying on each tool individually, you'll learn how to combine **these two powerful tools** to build optimized and timeless trading strategies. I've covered every important aspect in relation to Elliott Wave and Fibonacci topics in great detail and in a simple manner so that you can grasp them easily and systematically.

I've been trading for a living for more than 10 years now and I've successfully built some long-term effective trading strategies in the financial markets. I've been a big fan of both Elliott Wave and Fibonacci tools for long, partly because of their power in anticipating price movement instead of lagging behind price reactions. This urges me to release my first book about the magical duo in the trading endeavor. Whether in forex, commodities, equities, or crypto, the strategies I present in this book will immensely help you with filtering high-probability trade setups. You will find some "aha" moments that you've been waiting for long. By the end of this book, you'll have everything you'll need about trading with the Elliott Wave principle and four magical Fibonacci tools.

The most valuable asset in our lives is *time*. Unless you take determined steps in changing the way you approach trading in a more comprehensive way, you can easily be undermined by a lot of failures and negative feelings. If you are unfamiliar with these two "popular tools", you can be confident to absorb the information inside because I've tried to present them in a specific manner with many useful notes. Through a lot of real examples with detailed analysis, you can easily get what I convey even if you are a complete newbie. For those of you who have used the tools to some extent but cannot benefit much from them, or haven't tried to combine them the most effective way, this book will help you to rearrange everything about detecting and timing trades systematically and effectively in the markets based on proven models. Remember this book focuses on **high probability trades** only, and there is no room for mediocre ones.

In this book, I'll start to introduce every aspect of the Elliott Wave principle and Fibonacci tools to help you gain a comprehensive understanding of the topics. Next, you'll learn the magical relationships between them in each progression of the wave. The last chapters would be the ones you expect the most where I've incorporated a lot of trading strategies in connection with each crucial topic that we cover during the earlier chapters of the book. You'll be amazed at how the strategies can help you master the wave reading and market timing in the market. Also, you'll have the chance to learn a number of effective indicators and tools employed in each strategy to identify the very best trade setups.

Now, if you're ready, let's get started.

# CHAPTER 1: ELLIOTT WAVE FOUNDATIONS

## Elliott Wave Principle

Ralph Nelson Elliott (28 July 1871 – 15 January 1948) was the originator of the Elliott Wave theory. During his time working overseas, he was forced to take early retirement due to his illness. It was during those times that he began to study around 75 years of financial market data, particularly the U.S stock market. As you can imagine, during the period, price data wasn't easy to access due to the lack of Internet. But he was able to go back to the mid-1850s to collect them. That is definitely a huge effort by Ralph Nelson Elliott.

During his study, Elliott discovered persistent and repeating patterns that appeared between tops and bottoms and then theorized them into "Waves". Wave analysis helps analysts to predict high probability market turns. After testing the theory for over four years, he summarized his research in a book titled "The Wave Principle".

According to Elliott, although price movements appeared to be random and unpredictable on the surface, they follow predictable, natural laws and reflected the psychology of mass investors. Once we understand this concept and learn how the patterns contained within the waves behave, we can apply it to the markets to gain a tremendous edge in our trading. Also, with "The Wave Principle", he not only introduced profound discoveries about market behaviors but was also able to take it one step further by converging the Fibonacci sequence of numbers into the theory.

One last note, although he used the U.S stock market data for his studies, the principles behind the Elliott Wave concept can be applied to any freely traded markets, including but not limited to stocks, commodities, forex, or crypto.

## Market structure

Our basic understanding of market structure should begin with an introduction to the concept of fractals. Essentially, a fractal is a geometric shape that repeats its pattern at varying scales. Think of it as a pattern within a pattern within a pattern, and so on. Benoit Mandelbrot was a famous mathematician who did a lot of fractal analysis in the mid-1970s. He describes the fractal as being a geometric shape that when divided into parts, each part would be a smaller replica of the whole shape.

Let's take a look at a few examples of fractals that'll help convey this concept better.

Trees are one of the most quintessential fractals in nature. As they grow, branches develop from the trunk, and each of these branches develops smaller branches. You can notice the repetition of the Y shape throughout the trees if you look closely at any complex trees. These fractal designs help lower branches to increase their exposure to the sunshine.

The sunflower is also an example of fractals in our natural environment. A sunflower plant creates its pattern through a repetitive process. It starts out with just one seed, then shifts at a particular angle and creates another seed, and the process rotates again.

Foam is another example of fractals in action. The foam on your morning latte is fractal. In nature, bubbles can occur where raindrops have fallen or when ocean waves break, creating self-similar patterns. Large bubbles intersperse with smaller bubbles which will then intersperse with even smaller bubbles, and so forth.

These three examples are just the tip of the iceberg. Our natural world is filled with fractals. Rivers around the world are fractal in nature. Leaves are fractal. Ice and snow are fractal. Even our DNA has fractal characteristics.

Now, you may be wondering: Well, that's all fine, but what does all this have anything to do with the markets?

It may surprise you, but even the financial markets are fractal in nature, and this concept is critical to understanding the underlying structure of the market. The Elliott Wave theory lays out this fractal market structure in a very clear and detailed manner.

Let's take a look at one complete Elliott Wave cycle consisting of eight waves below.

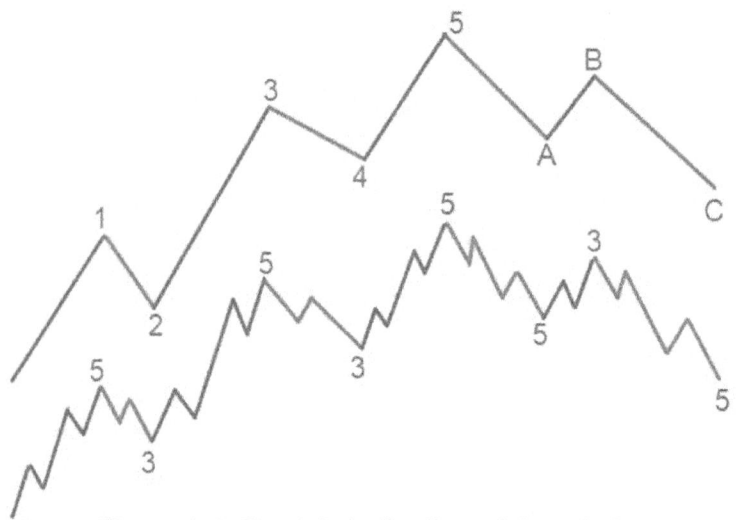

Figure 1-1: Fractals in the financial markets

As you can see, the five waves that occur within the motive sequence are labeled 1, 2, 3, 4, and 5, and the three waves that occur within the corrective sequence are labeled A, B, and C. There are eight waves in total in an entire cycle. This structure is the building block for all waves. Essentially, the structure will repeat itself in all degrees. We see repeating patterns connected to each other at different frequencies or time frames. Waves are embedded within waves. As such, the structure of the market is set to be fractal.

To grasp this in more simplistic terms, think about a price chart. If you look at any chart, can you tell whether it's a monthly chart, a weekly chart, a daily chart, or any other type of chart? You can't. The price action on the chart alone cannot tell you what the time frame is due to the fractal nature of wave structures within the market. Our actions in the market leave behind a footprint that is embedded within the price charts.

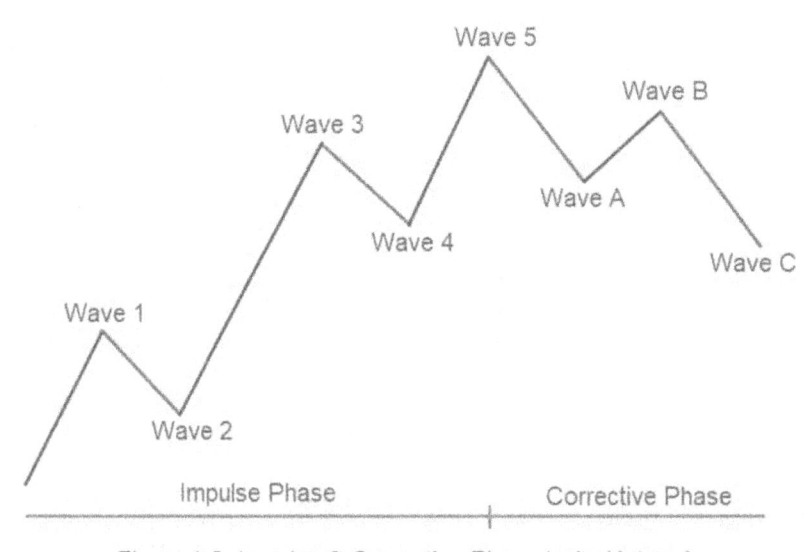

Figure 1-2: Impulse & Corrective Phase In An Uptrend

Let's turn our attention to a basic wave structure. In this example, we are looking at a bullish trend. You will notice that within the motive wave sequence, Waves 1, 3, and 5 move in the direction of the uptrend while Waves 2 and 4 make retracements against the main uptrend.

The corrective sequence follows the completion of Wave 5 and moves in the opposite direction. The correction is labeled A, B and C. Notice Waves A and C move against the motive sequence while the intermediary wave (Wave B) moves counter to Waves A and C.

Now let's see how this works in a downtrend.

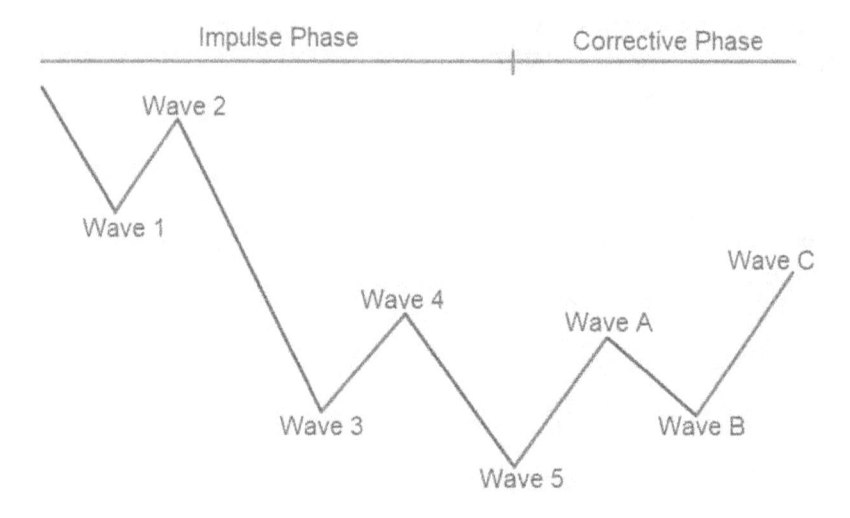

Figure 1-3: Impulse & Corrective Phase In A Downtrend

In this diagram, you can see that within the motive wave sequence, Waves 1, 3, and 5 move in the direction of the prevailing downtrend while Waves 2 and 4 interrupt those advances and move counter to the main downtrend. The corrective sequence follows the completion of Wave 5 and moves in the opposite direction. The correction is labeled A, B, and C. Notice how Waves A and C move counter to the motive sequence while the intermediary wave (Wave B) moves counter to Waves A and C.

This is the basic underlying structure of the markets regardless of the time frame that you analyze. It's important that you really understand the market structure as everything else will build upon this.

## **Wave Psychology**

A wave cycle represents mass crowd behavior in the financial markets. By studying the wave patterns, we can better understand where the price is in relation to the overall market cycle so that we can gain an edge in extracting profits from the markets. Unlike the efficient market hypothesis which essentially states that neither technical nor fundamental analysis can work consistently in the market, we, as technical analysts, know that traders can gain a consistent edge in the market by using the right timing tools.

The Elliott Wave theory supports the idea that market participants are not always rational and that their decisions in the market are not entirely driven by logic. In other words, emotions tend to play a large part in the investment decision process.

Let's take a look at how human emotions drive market prices by studying the psychology of market participants at different waves within the cycle. Specifically, we'll look at what happens after a sustained downtrend.

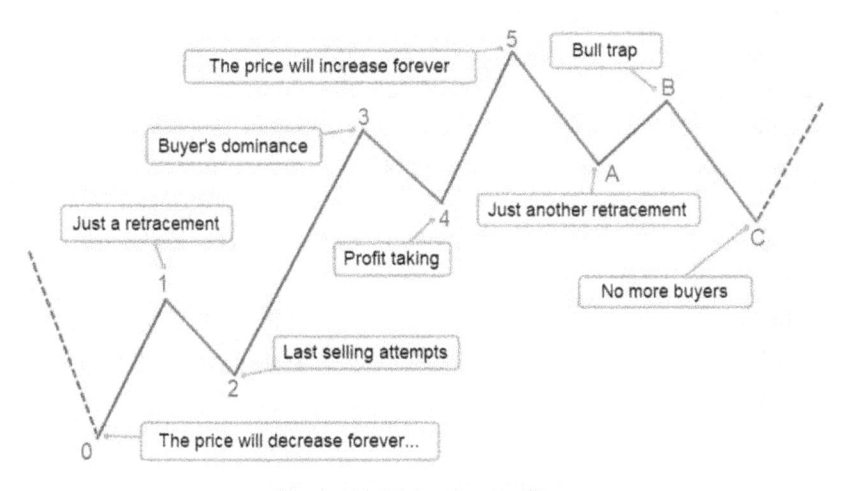

Figure 1-4: Wave personalities

## Waves 1 and 2

The start of Wave 1 begins after the market has been in a sustained downtrend for some time and the fundamental outlook is still negative. In fact, there are no more sellers left to drive the market lower, and as such, the price begins to move higher. However, this is interpreted as a temporary correction in a bearish market by many traders, and they believe the downtrend will soon continue. Due to this psychological aspect, we can expect Wave 2 to be a relatively sharp and deep retracement of Wave 1.

Wave 3
---

The selling pressure has now reached its exhaustion point and buying demand begins to overwhelm supply. The fundamental outlook begins to look a little better and there can be some positive economic news or events that occur at this stage. As a result, optimism begins to build. Once the peak of Wave 1 has been taken out, more and more investors are aware of the trend reversal and hop on the new bandwagon. They start to liquidate their shorts and start taking on more long positions. This increased buying interest is evident in the steep slope and strong momentum that is characteristic of Wave 3 price action. Wave 3 is typically the longest wave in the cycle that offers the best profit potential.

Wave 4
---

By the end of Wave 3, there is no mistaking the uptrend. Optimism begins to permeate the market. This is followed by Wave 4 which is typically a relatively long drawn-out wave. In Wave 4, traders/investors who got in early during Waves 1 and 3 are now sitting on a healthy amount of profit, and they begin to liquidate some of their positions to lock in those profits. This activity leaves behind a sideways price action footprint that is often seen in Wave 4. The volatility also drives up during this wave. It is during Wave 4 that many trend following systems get whipsawed by false signals, resulting in a series of losing trades. The price is range bound and it feels as if the market isn't going anywhere anytime soon.

Wave 5
---

Contrary to what many traders may think, the market is poised to move higher as Wave 5 starts and prices begin to rebound. The retail public becomes more and more interested and they fuel this last leg higher. The news headlines are filled with positive stories, and even your average mom-and-pop investors are talking about the markets at their dinner parties. The signs of an optimistic mass herd mentality are everywhere. The price action in Wave 5 tends to be more sluggish than in Wave 3, and there may be a divergence pattern between Wave 3 and Wave 5. This is because the momentum of the price rise is raining and there are now fewer investors that are sitting on the sidelines. The commercials and institutions got aboard the trend early during Wave 1 and 3, and the retail public jumped on the bandwagon later during the Wave 5 progression. Now, there's no one left to push prices higher.

## Wave A

The tide is set to shift. When Wave 5 ends, it brings an end to the impulse sequence and reigns in the corrective wave sequence. Wave A kicks off the sequence as it retraces a large portion of Wave 5. In most times, the price action in Wave A is sharp. Most traders, however, aren't concerned at this point. They see it as just another pullback - an opportunity to add to their long positions.

## Wave B

This newfound buying demand drives prices higher in Wave B, but Wave B is a bull trap that will eventually draw in the crowd and catch them on the wrong side of the market. Professionals will begin to see the shifting tide and position themselves on the short side. They will take the other side of the order flow, against the retail public who are in euphoric mode at this time. Crushing the hopes of many, Wave B will be a short-lived affair and will not push the current trend higher. Instead, it will result in the emergence of Wave C to the downside.

## Wave C

This wave has many characteristics of Wave 3. It is Wave C that convinces the bulls that the uptrend is finally over. A complete realization of this will come as the swing low of Wave A has been taken out. When this realization strikes, those bulls who have been caught on the wrong side of the market will act to redeem themselves and join other new shorts. Most traders will now believe that the previous bull market has ended as they increasingly position on the short side. The shorts may realize some profits as Wave C progresses. However, just when they begin to gain confidence in their position, the market will again reverse to the upside as it completes Wave C and repeats the cycle all over again. Unfortunately, the cruelty of the market never ends for many uninformed traders who don't understand the underlying structure of the market.

We've discovered some basic yet crucial concepts of the Elliott Wave theory and its different waves in both the impulse and corrective phases. All in all, the markets are driven by human emotions, and this leaves a certain footprint that the trained eyes can spot and take advantage of. When we know what this cycle looks like on the price chart and the market psychology behind it, we can confidently position ourselves to make use of instead of being a victim of the price moves. In the following chapter, we'll go over the first type of wave: ***the motive wave***.

# CHAPTER 2: MOTIVE WAVES

## Elliott Wave Cycle

To start with, let's talk about **wave cycles**. Wave cycles can be classified into two different categories: **motive waves** and **corrective waves**. While motive waves move in the direction of the larger trend, corrective waves move contrary to the larger trend.

There are two types of motive waves: *impulses* and *diagonals*, and diagonals can be further segmented into *leading* and *ending diagonals*.

Impulse waves are the most common type of motive waves. Both impulses and diagonal waves move in the direction of the larger trend. However, there are different rules that apply to each type. In this chapter, we'll be focusing on the rules for both of these types.

## Impulse Wave

An *impulse wave* pattern indicates a strong price move in the direction of the prevailing trend. Impulse waves refer to upward movements in an uptrend and downward movements in a downtrend. Let's take a look at an impulse waveform in the illustration below.

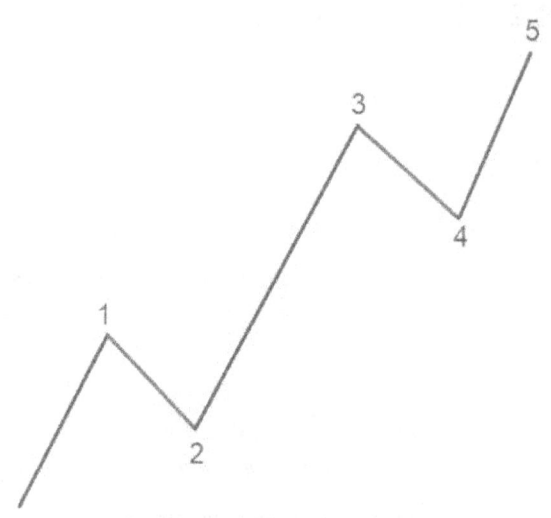

Figure 2-1: Impulse Wave

An impulse wave is comprised of five sub-waves that make net movement in the same direction of the trend of the next larger degree. Among the five sub-waves, three of them are motive waves as well, and the remaining two waves are corrective by nature.

The impulse wave is the most common type of motive wave and can be found in Wave 1, 3, and 5 of the impulse sequence. In most cases, we can start an impulse wave count at a significantly higher low. However, this is not always the case as we will see later when discussing truncations. But for the most part, this guideline for starting wave counts will often hold TRUE.

Let's look at some impulse waves on a price chart.

Figure 2-2: Impulse Wave In An Uptrend

On this chart, we have a bullish GBP/USD price chart on the 4-hour time frame. Starting from the swing low, prices move upward to form Wave 1 before retracing to form Wave 2. Afterward, we can see strong momentum in Wave 3, followed by a shallow pullback in Wave 4, and a final push to higher highs in Wave 5. Notice how Waves 3 and 5 in this example also carve out a five-wave structure of a smaller degree.

Let's take a look at an example of an impulse form on a bearish price chart.

Figure 2-3: Impulse Wave In A Downtrend

This is the daily chart of Gold. Starting from the swing high, the price moves down to form Wave 1. Then, we see a deep retracement in Wave 2. After that, the price starts to move sharply lower in Wave 3, followed by overlapping price action in Wave 4. Finally, there's one more push to the downside in Wave 5, which takes out the low of Wave 3 to complete the impulse sequence. In this example, Wave 3 and 5 also carve out a five-wave structure of a smaller degree.

The Elliott Wave principle has three unbreakable rules in connection with impulse waves:

1. Wave 2 cannot retrace more than 100 percent of Wave 1;
2. Wave 3 cannot be the shortest wave;
3. Wave 4 cannot enter into the price territory of Wave 1.

These are three hard and fast rules when it comes to applying the Elliott Wave principle within the impulse wave.

Now let's take a closer look at the impulse structure from the lens of the three unbreakable rules within the Elliott Wave theory.

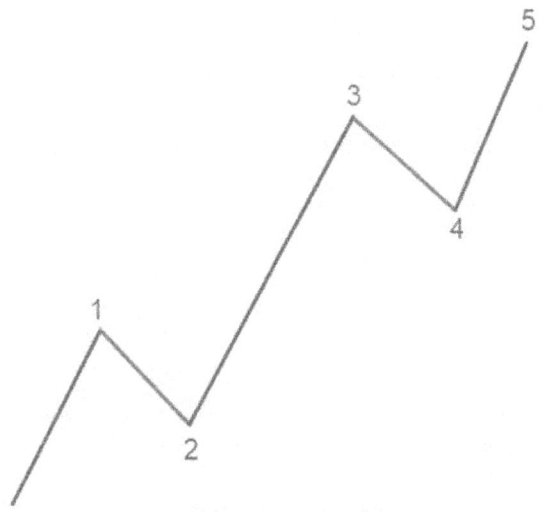

Figure 2-4: Impulse Wave

The first rule for impulse waves is *Wave 2 cannot retrace more than 100 percent of Wave 1*. Obviously, we can see that Wave 2 did not breach the beginning of Wave 1, so the first rule has been adhered to. Next, *Wave 3 cannot be the shortest wave*. It's important to note that Wave 3 doesn't have to be the longest wave in the impulse sequence, but it cannot be the shortest. We can confirm from this diagram that Wave 3 is not the shortest wave within the impulse sequence. Finally, *Wave 4 cannot enter into the price territory of Wave 1*. In this example, we can see that the low of Wave 4 is well above the high of Wave 1. Therefore, we can confirm that this waveform satisfies all the conditions of a typical impulse wave.

From my experience, violating any of these three rules, even in the slightest, can lead to inferior trades.

## Guidelines on impulse waves

Now that we've discussed the primary rules for Elliott Wave, let's talk about some of the guidelines. But first, it's important to understand the difference between rules and guidelines. Again, a rule in the context of Elliott Wave theory cannot be broken. A guideline, on the other hand, is a tendency. It is a characteristic trait that often occurs but there's no requirement for it to exist. Yet, guidelines are extremely helpful in navigating the wave structure. Let's go over the three most important guidelines within the impulse wave context.

1. Wave 3 is often the strongest wave

Wave 3 will typically be the strongest wave with the steepest slope and highest amount of momentum behind. This guideline has a very strong tendency when it comes to the forex and equities markets. In the commodities markets, however, we often see Wave 5 being the strongest wave.

2. Waves 1 and 5 tend toward equality

Basically, the length of Wave 1 will be relatively equal to the length of Wave 5. When Wave 3 is the longest wave, which is typically the case in the forex and equity market, we can expect Wave 1 and 5 to be of similar length. This is quite useful to know as it can provide us with insight into the probable termination point for Wave 5. Basically, we can project the length of Wave 1 off the end of Wave 4 to get an approximate ending point for Wave 5.

3. If Wave 2 is a simple sharp correction, Wave 4 will most likely be a simple sideways correction or complex sideways correction

We will be able to better understand this guideline once we have gone over different types of corrective structures in the next chapter. However, for now, it's important to understand that the corrective waves within the impulse sequence (Waves 2 and 4) tend to have different characteristics. There is a strong tendency for Wave 2 to be a deep sharp correction and for Wave 4 to be a shallower and more prolonged correction. This has to do with the psychology of the market participants in Wave 2 versus Wave 4. Remember during Wave 2, traders and investors are expecting continued pressure in the direction of the trend which leads to a sharp retracement. Whereas, in Wave 4 there's more profit-taking going on and the movement is less aggressive, which leads to a sideways and shallow retracement.

There are many interesting points in studying the Elliott Wave principle. Below are some other rules and guidelines that can be very helpful in price movement analysis.

Additional rules

- Wave 1 can either be an impulse or a leading diagonal.
- Wave 5 can either be an impulse or an ending diagonal.

Note: We will be talking more about leading and ending diagonals in the next section.

Additional guidelines

- Waves 1, 3, and 5 tend to subdivide into 5 waves.
- In some rare cases, Wave 5 will fail to move beyond Wave 3. This is referred to as a truncation (we will learn in the next section).
- Wave 3 is **most likely** to extend, followed by Wave 5.
- The length of Wave 3 is often 161 percent of Wave 1.
- Wave 5 often ends at the trend line drawn from Waves 1 or 3 that is parallel to the trend line connecting the ends of Waves 2 and 4.

Again, we still have to go over some of these concepts including truncations, extensions, and parallel trend lines. Once we do so, these guidelines will become much clearer to you. But it's important that I include them here for the sake of completeness.

## **Diagonal Waves**

### Leading Diagonals

A *leading diagonal* is a wave structure that can be found in the first wave within a regular five-wave impulse (Wave 1) or at the beginning of the corrective sequence (Wave A). A leading diagonal shares some similarities with an impulse wave, including the five-wave structure. However, it differs from an impulse wave in some points.

Here are the two key differences.

- Wave 1 within the leading diagonal tends to be the largest leg within the structure;
- Waves 2 and 4 of a leading diagonal should overlap.

If you recall from the previous section on the impulse wave structure, Wave 3 tends to be the largest wave within the impulse sequence, and Waves 2 and 4 cannot overlap. These are two important distinguishing factors between impulses and diagonals.

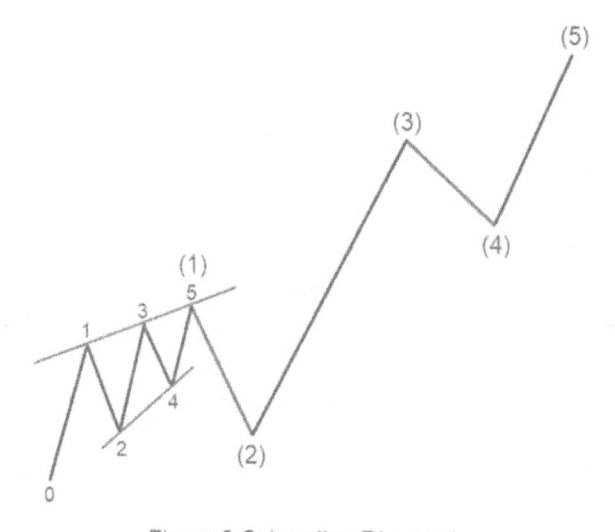

Figure 2-5: Leading Diagonal

In this diagram, we have a leading diagonal of a contracting variety. If you take a close look at this illustration and turn your attention to the sub-waves within Wave 1, you'll see the five legs that make up the leading diagonal. In addition, you'll notice that the first leg of the leading diagonal is the largest one, and Waves 2 and 4 overlap. A trend line can be drawn connecting Waves 1 and 3 on one side, and Waves 2 and 4 on the other side. Both lines in this example are converging as they progress, creating a contracting diagonal. If, however, the two trend lines were diverging from one another, then we would call it an expanding diagonal.

Leading diagonals carry the same meaning as the impulse waves, indicating the direction of the larger trend. They typically take longer to trace out their path than do impulses which can cover a lot of ground in a short span of time. Once the leading diagonal formation is complete, the price action will progress to form Wave 2 of the impulse sequence or Wave B of the corrective sequence.

Now, let's see what a leading diagonal looks like on a real price chart:

Figure 2-6: Leading Diagonal Structure

This is the daily chart of the Aussie/US Dollar pair. The first wave of this 5-wave impulse downtrend is a leading diagonal which consists of five sub-waves marked 1-2-3-4-5. Notice we have a channel that is contracting by nature, and each wave within the channel seems to be larger than the following one. After completing this diagonal formation, the Gold price retraced a bit to form Wave 2 and then fell sharply afterward in Waves 3 and 5.

## Ending diagonals

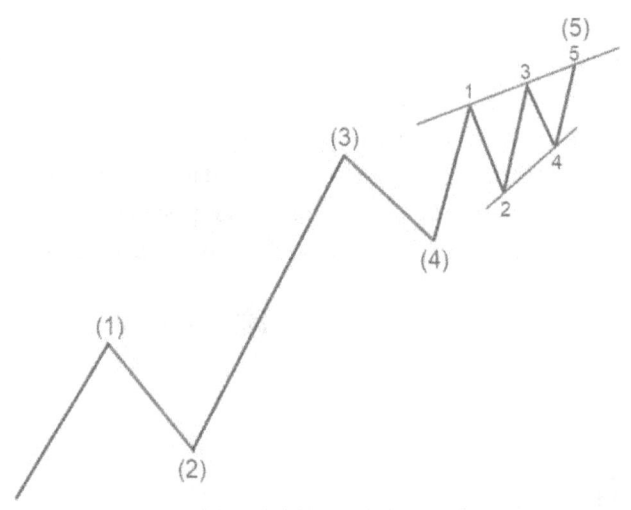

Figure 2-7: Ending Diagonal

Now let's turn our attention to the second class of diagonals: ***the ending diagonal.*** An ending diagonal, as the name suggests, is a wave structure that can be found at the end of the five-wave impulse sequence (Wave 5) or at the end of the A-B-C correction (Wave C). Ending diagonals are more prevalent than leading diagonals. Traditional technical analysts recognize this pattern as a wedge formation occurring during the late stages of a trend. Ending diagonals offer an excellent trading opportunity for those that can spot its progression within the cycle. Typically, we will see a swift reaction in the opposite direction of the overall trend once the 2-4 trend line of the diagonal has been broken. At that time, we want to ride the momentum following that breakout.

As with leading diagonals, ending diagonals are also comprised of five waves labeled 1 through 5. Additionally, Wave 1 within the ending diagonal tends to be the largest leg within the structure while Waves 2 and 4 of the ending diagonal should overlap. Often, we will see prices shoot beyond the trend line connecting Waves 1 and 3 within the ending diagonal. This is referred to as a throwover. It's when the market makes one last push before the tide finally turns and the price action subsequently reverses.

One question that often arises with respect to diagonals is "Do the leading or ending diagonal have to exist within the 5-3 structure?".

The answer is "No".

Leading diagonals can occur in Wave 1 or Wave A as we mentioned. However, there is no requirement for it to exist, and in fact, it will not be present within the overall structure in most cases. The same goes for ending diagonals.

Figure 2-8: Ending Diagonal Structure

In this example, we have a price chart of the Aussie/Japanese Yen pair on the 4-hour time frame. Notice that after a strong decline in Wave 3 and a minor pullback into Wave 4, prices began to consolidate as they moved lower. This type of price action in the late stages of the trend can often clue us into the possibility of an ending diagonal in progress. We can see Wave 1 of the ending diagonal has the largest leg within the structure, and Waves 2 and 4 overlap. Soon after, prices began to reverse and a solid buying opportunity would exist at the upside break of the 2-4 diagonal trend line.

## Subdivision

Now that we understand the difference between a leading and ending diagonal, let's take a look at the inner structure of each.

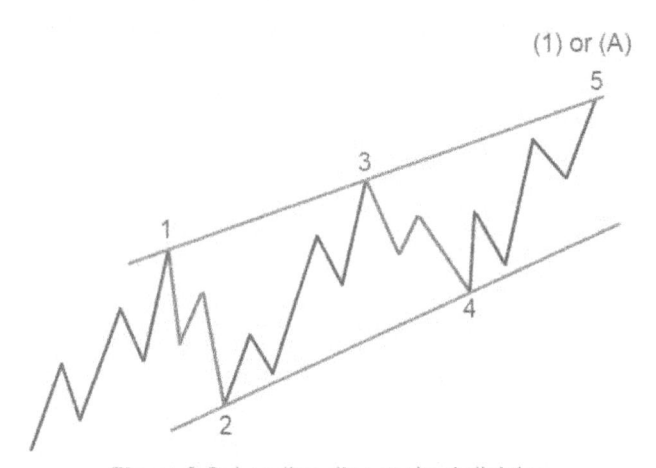

*Figure 2-9: Leading diagonal subdivision*

We'll start with the leading diagonal. The leading diagonal has a 5-3-5-3-5 internal wave structure, meaning that:

- The first, third, and fifth legs subdivide into five waves of a smaller degree.
- The second and fourth legs subdivide into three waves of a smaller degree.

The impulse wave structure we discussed in the previous section is also a 5-3-5-3-5 structure. Note the higher degree wave is labeled (1) or (A) because we know that a leading diagonal can only occur in these two positions.

Now let's turn our attention to the ending diagonal subdivision.

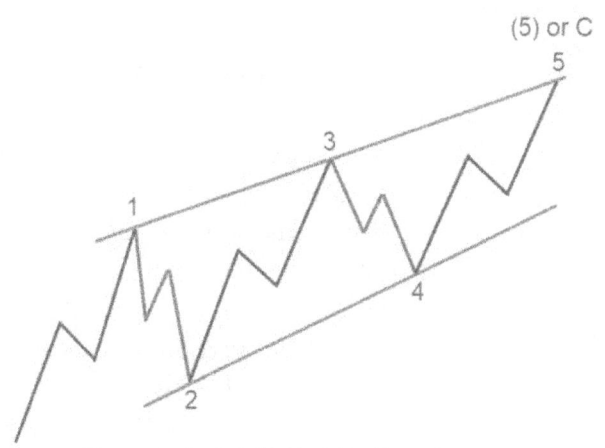

Figure 2-10: Ending diagonal subdivision

Comparing this structure to the leading diagonal, what seems to stand out the most? Well, if you said the subdivisions look different, then you would be absolutely right. The ending diagonal has a 3-3-3-3-3 internal wave structure, meaning that every leg within the structure subdivides into three smaller waves. Typically, each of these subdivisions is a simple A-B-C zigzag. Note that the higher degree wave is labeled (5) or (C) in this case as we know that an ending diagonal can only occur in the Wave (5) or Wave (C) position.

Now, let's recap some of the rules and guidelines for diagonal waves that we've discussed so far so that we can help solidify these concepts within our minds.

<u>Rules for diagonal waves:</u>

- Leading diagonals can appear in Wave (1) or Wave (A);
- Ending diagonals can appear in Wave (5) or Wave (C);
- Diagonals subdivide into 5 waves;
- Each wave of an ending diagonal subdivides into 3 smaller waves;
- Waves 1 and 4 overlap.

Guidelines for diagonal waves:

- Wave 1 tends to be the largest wave among Waves 1, 3, and 5 in both leading and ending diagonals;
- A leading diagonal often subdivides into a 5-3-5-3-5 structure;
- In a contracting diagonal, Wave 5 often terminates slightly beyond the trend line connecting Waves 1 and 3 of the diagonal;
- In an expanding diagonal, Wave 5 often terminates slightly before the trend line connecting Waves 1 and 3 of the diagonal;
- If Wave 1 is a leading diagonal or Wave 5 is an ending diagonal, then Wave 3 will most likely be the extended wave.

## Truncations and Extensions

Truncation

As we've learned from the section on impulse waves, Wave 5 of an impulse typically takes out the extreme of Wave 3. However, sometimes Wave 5 fails to do so. When this happens, it is referred to as a 5th wave failure or simply a **truncation**.

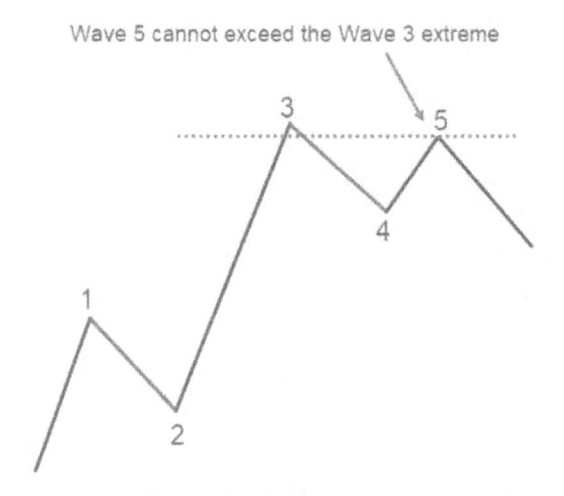

Figure 2-11: Truncation

This diagram shows what a truncation looks like. Notice that Wave 5 fails to extend beyond the top of Wave 3. In traditional technical analysis, this often resembles a *double top* in an uptrend and a *double bottom* in a downtrend.

Even though Wave 5 is truncated, its subdivisions will still hold. By that, I mean this Wave 5 still subdivides into five smaller waves. Truncated fifth waves are among the trickiest part of the Elliott Wave principle. The biggest challenge is that you cannot predict a truncation. You can only guess. However, the fact that a truncated Wave 5 happens once in a hundred times makes guessing meaningless. I would say that 9 out of 10 times, what appears to be a truncated fifth wave is really just the early stages of a normal fifth wave. Hence, a trader needs to be very careful in making this classification. Here's a real example of a fifth wave failure or truncation as it's commonly called.

Figure 2-12: Truncation

This truncation occurred in the Pound Sterling/Swiss Franc pair on the 1-hour chart. Until Wave 4, it appears that the price action is moving along a normal impulse wave sequence. As prices began to move higher in Wave 5, there was one attempt to get beyond the Wave 3 extreme without success. Notice the long wick in the last candle within Wave 5 which managed to touch the Wave

3 high before strongly reversing to the downside. Hence, we can confirm a truncated Wave 5 in this example.

Extensions

***Extension*** is another important topic relating to impulse waves. Unlike truncations that fall short of their minimum expected price projection, extensions, on the other hand, are waves that appear to be elongated or excessive in length. Though extensions can appear in any of the impulse Waves 1, 3, or 5, the most common extended wave is Wave 3. When an extension is present, it often appears as a 9-wave formation within the overall 5-wave impulse sequence. Also, Wave 3 of 3 will register the highest momentum within the overall structure.

Figure 2-13: Extension

Take a look at this diagram. This is an example of a third wave extension. In this case, we have a total of 13 waves within the overall structure. You can often see a series of ones and twos being labeled at the beginning of the structure.

Now, let's visually compare extensions at different impulse wave positions.

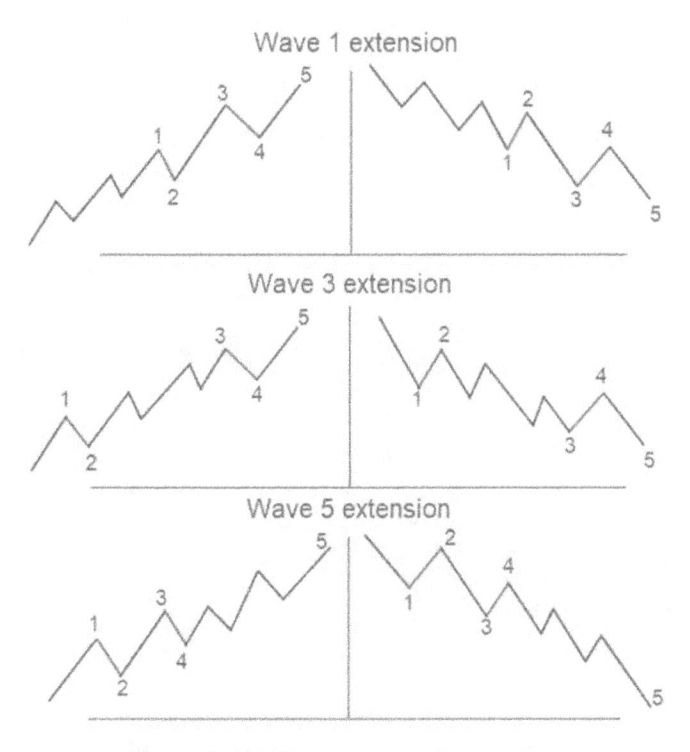

Figure 2-14: Comparison of extensions

The top diagram shows what a first wave extension looks like in an up and down market. Notice how the first wave subdivides into five smaller waves and is the longest wave in the impulse sequence. Also, the first wave is the least likely to extend.

The second diagram illustrates what a third wave extension looks like. Note that the minimum extension for an extended Wave 3 is 161.8 percent of Wave 1 added to the end of Wave 2. As we've mentioned several times, Wave 3 is the most likely to be extended within the impulse phase. While we cannot put this exactly in percentages, I would say more than 70 percent of extensions occur in the Wave 3 position.

Finally, the last diagram displays a fifth wave extension. It is the second most likely wave to be extended. In this scenario, the price in the next Wave (Wave A) may often retrace a minimum of 61.8 percent of the length of the fifth wave after the impulse sequence is complete. Notice that the structure for all three can be seen as a nine-wave sequence from start to end.

Let's now look at some real examples of extensions.

Figure 2-15: Wave 3 extension

This chart displays a third wave extension in the Gold price. Notice how Wave (3) is the largest wave in the intermediate degree sequence. It is the extended wave and its subdivision is clearly marked 1 through 5.

Let's take a look at another example of an extended fifth wave. Remember an extension in Wave 5 is seen more in commodities than in other markets, particularly on the daily and weekly charts.

Figure 2-16: Wave 5 extension

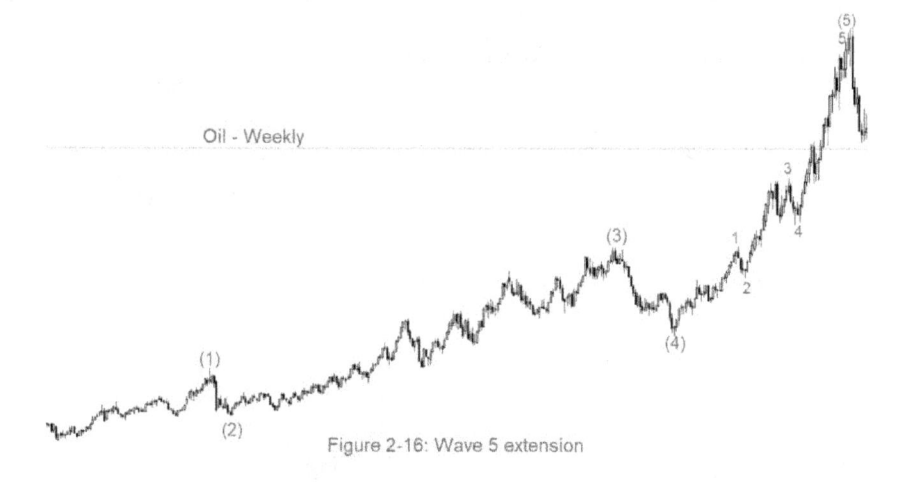

In this example, we have a weekly chart of crude oil. The fifth wave extension is quite obvious on this chart. The price action went parabolic in the late stages of this uptrend in Wave 5. The subdivisions are marked within Wave (5). In fact, if you look closely at Wave 5 within the larger Wave (5), you'll notice that it is also the extended wave within the impulse sequence.

Wave naming
---

Let's shift gears a bit and discuss some *labeling conventions* as it pertains to Elliott waves. As you know by now, the markets are fractal in nature, and waves of larger degrees are composed of waves of smaller degrees. This occurs in the market across all degrees from the yearly charts all the way down to the hourly and minute charts. As you might imagine, it's quite difficult for the Elliott Wave analysts to articulate the degree of the trend without some types of labeling convention. Thankfully, there is a labeling system that many Elliott Wave users use. Starting from the largest degree of trend, we have nine designations as follows:

| Wave Degree | 5s With the Trend | 3s Against the Trend |
|---|---|---|
| | (↑ next is Arabic symbols) | (↑ next is caps) |
| Grand Supercycle | Ⓘ Ⓘ Ⓘ Ⓘ Ⓥ | ⓐ ⓑ ⓒ |
| Supercycle | (I) (II) (III) (IV) (V) | (a) (b) (c) |
| Cycle | I II III IV V | a b c |
| Primary | ① ② ③ ④ ⑤ | Ⓐ Ⓑ Ⓒ |
| Intermediate | (1) (2) (3) (4) (5) | (A) (B) (C) |
| Minor | 1 2 3 4 5 | A B C |
| Minute | ⓘ ⓘ ⓘ ⓘ ⓥ | ⓐ ⓑ ⓒ |
| Minuette | (i) (ii) (iii) (iv) (v) | (a) (b) (c) |
| Subminuette | i ii iii iv v | a b c |
| | (↓ next is Arabic symbols) | (↓ next is caps) |

Figure 2-17: Wave naming (source: bullwaves.org)

Next to each designation, you can see the impulse wave and corrective wave labels.

At first sight, this labeling system might seem quite overwhelming, but you'll be happy to know that you don't really need to memorize this labeling system. Practically speaking, when we're trading, we're not concerned with every degree of trend. It's more important to understand the essential concepts behind impulsive and corrective waves. Impulse waves are labeled 1, 2, 3, 4, 5, and corrective waves are labeled A, B, and C.

Until now, we've covered a lot of aspects regarding motive waves which include impulses and diagonals. In the following chapter, we'll be diving into everything you'll need to know about corrective waves. I hope you're ready for that.

# CHAPTER 3: CORRECTIVE WAVES

## Corrective Phase

The Elliott Wave principle provides a roadmap for market movements. Once we understand what this roadmap looks like, we can take advantage of these price movements within various wave cycles. So far, we've discussed the motive wave structure which is further segmented into impulse wave and diagonal wave. We should also know that every five-wave motive sequence is followed by a three-wave corrective sequence.

Keep in mind that the friction and pressure from the higher degree trend prevent a corrective structure from turning into an impulsive one.

Think of this as a tug of war where the larger degree trend is exerting significantly higher pressure on prices than the corrective phase. Even though the corrective phase can slow down the progression of the trend, it will eventually be influenced by the overall cyclical pressure of the higher degree trend. Many types of trend-following strategies do very well during the impulsive phase but they tend to give back a large portion of their profits during the corrective phase. Those strategies tend to make the most amount of money when they are lucky enough to catch the extended wave within the impulse sequence. However, these strategies inevitably fall on tough times during corrections as they tend to get whipsawed to death, giving back most if not all of their profits.

Why does this happen so often to trend followers? Remember that tradable trends exist only about 30 percent of the time. Most of the time, the markets are just consolidating in a corrective phase. Pure trend-following strategies are more reactive than predictive. Hence, they tend to be late to enter and exit. The Elliott Wave principle, on the other hand, offers a valuable framework for understanding predictive market movements. It tells us when we should be in and out of the market. We can gain a valuable edge that 90 percent of traders don't.

In this chapter, we'll start diving into corrective structures. It's extremely important that we understand the different corrective patterns. Keep in mind that most tradable opportunities will occur at the end of a corrective pattern in an attempt to catch the next impulse move. Yet, it is challenging at times to find the end of the corrective sequence as there are many different variations. As we move forward, we'll see that there are certain rules and guidelines that can help us along the way. The more that we learn about corrective structures, the better prepared we will be in positioning ourselves for the next move in the market.

## Types Of Corrective Patterns

Basically, there are two classes of corrective structures: **sharp corrections** and **sideways corrections**. As the name suggests, a sharp correction occurs when the price retraces quite deeply into the territory of the previous wave. On the other hand, a sideways correction happens when the price retracement is relatively shallow and prolonged.

In terms of the Elliott Wave principle, there are three types of corrective structures: **zigzags**, **flats**, and **triangles.** While the zigzag corrections fall into the sharp correction category, flats and triangles are in the sideways variety. Regardless of the type of corrective structure, they all act to interrupt the larger trend. Once the corrective form is complete, the price will continue to move in the direction of the dominating trend.

## Zigzag pattern

The **zigzag pattern** is the simplest and most prevalent type of corrective patterns in the market. The pattern resembles a lightning bolt on the price chart. The zigzag pattern moves opposite to the overall trend and is labeled A, B, and C. It often appears in the Wave 2 position after a prolonged price move. Traders are not convinced that a change in trend is imminent and view it as a minor correction within the larger trend. Because of this psychological tenet,

Wave 2 tends to form a sharp retracement in the form of a zigzag pattern. Let's take a look at some characteristics of a zigzag pattern in more detail.

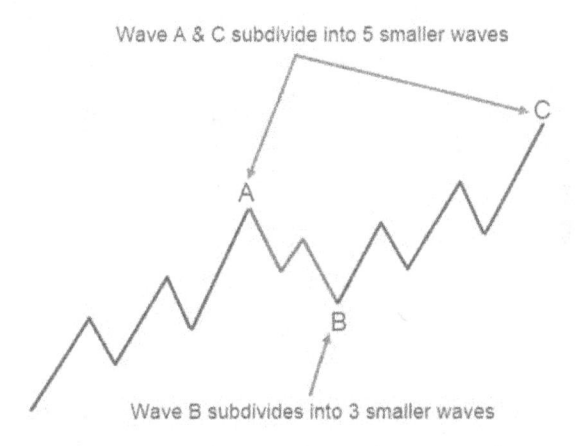

Figure 3-1: Zigzag pattern

The zigzag pattern consists of three legs labeled A, B, and C. The A-B-C pattern within a zigzag forms a 5-3-5 internal wave structure. Moreover, Waves A and C of a zigzag **tend toward equality,** and Wave B won't retrace more than 61.8 percent of Wave A. These characteristics are very useful to project both the start and the end of Wave C of a zigzag. Let's see what a zigzag looks like on a price chart.

Figure 3-2: Zigzag pattern

In the example above, the market has been in an uptrend for some time. You can find a downward correcting zigzag that moves from Wave 1 into Wave 2. Notice the A-B-C waves of the zigzag structure and note how Waves A and C are fairly comparable in length. Once Wave C reached the length of Wave A, we would expect prices to reverse and move in the direction of the longer-term trend which is up in this case.

## Flat patterns

The second type of corrective structure is referred to as **flats**.

There are three types of flat corrections: **regular flat, expanded flat**, and **running flat**. Of these types, the regular flat and expanded flat tend to be more prevalent while the running flat is the least common.

The type of flat is determined by how Waves B and C trace out their path within the overall structure. Flat corrections appear to have some similar qualities to zigzags, but there are some distinct differences. For example, unlike the zigzag which has a 5-3-5 internal waveform, a flat has a 3-3-5 internal waveform, hence the flat pattern trades as a corrective-corrective-impulsive pattern. Moreover, while zigzags are often found in the Wave 2 position of the impulse, flats are more commonly found in the Wave 4 position of the impulse.

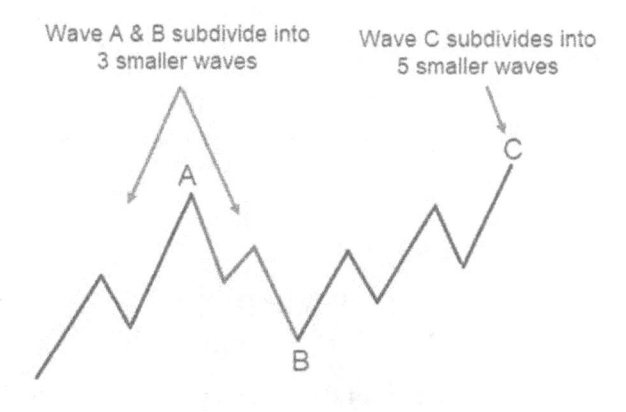

Figure 3-3: Flat pattern

Similar to zigzags, flats are composed of three waves labeled A, B, and C. Take a look at how Wave A and B subdivide into three waves. The final leg within the flat - Wave C - subdivides into five waves. If you notice that the first leg within the corrective structure (Wave A) is unfolding as a five-wave subdivision, you can expect an overall zigzag pattern. On the other hand, if you find that Wave A is a three-wave subdivision, you can be relatively certain that the corrective formation will either be a flat or a triangle (we will learn about triangles shortly).

Regular flat

Now, let's talk about the first type of flat correction - ***the regular flat.***

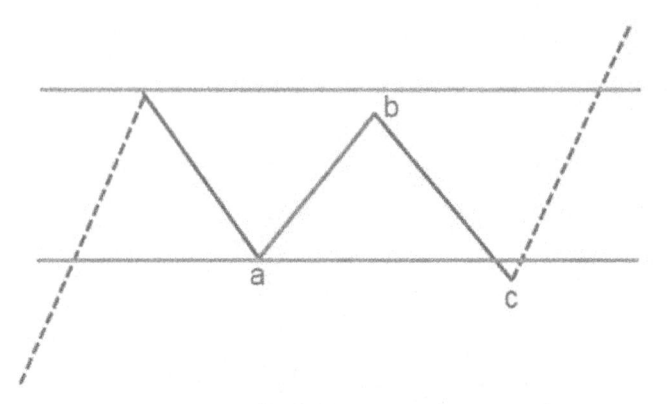

Figure 3-4: Regular flat

The regular flat is a common type of flat. Turning our attention to the diagram above which depicts an uptrend followed by a regular flat corrective structure, you'll notice some important characteristics of the regular flat. After the completion of Wave A, Wave B seems to inherit the lack of counter-trend momentum and terminates near the beginning of Wave A. A typical Wave B retracement would be at least 80 percent but not more than 100 percent of Wave A. In addition, Wave C will retrace the entire Wave B and extend slightly below it rather than significantly below as in zigzags.

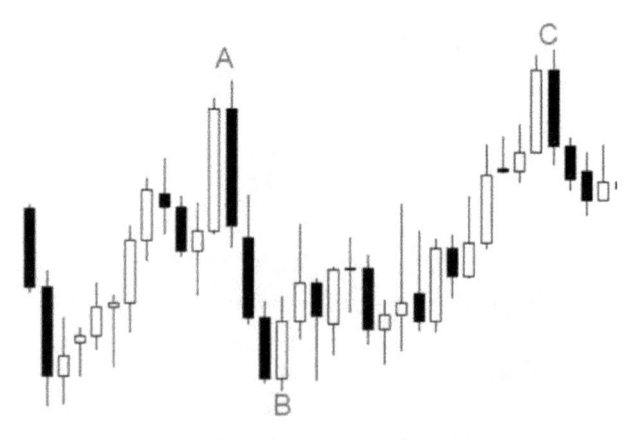

Figure 3-5: Regular flat pattern

Here's a chart showing an example of a regular flat correction in an overall bearish market. Notice how Wave B within this regular flat structure retraces more than 80 percent but less than 100 percent of Wave A. Also, Wave C terminates slightly beyond the end of Wave A in this example.

Expanding flat

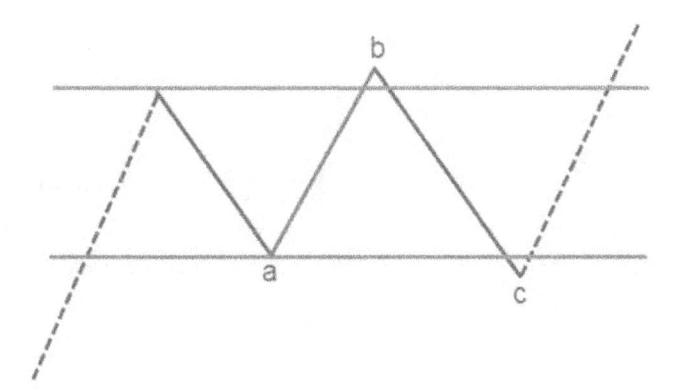

Figure 3-6: Expanding flat

Let's move on to the **expanding flat**. In this type of flat, Wave B retraces more than 100 percent of Wave A. This is the main difference between a regular flat and an expanding variation. Wave C travels below the end of Wave A, similar to the regular flat.

Expanding flats occur in a relatively strong market. The power behind the overall trend is so much that its inertia forces the price to move past the Wave A extreme during the Wave B formation. Let's turn our attention to this expanded flat correction in a downtrend.

Figure 3-7: Expanding flat pattern

This example illustrates an expanding flat in a downtrend. Notice how Wave B extends below Wave A and then moves higher to form Wave C, which takes out the high of Wave A. If you look closely at the substructure of Wave C, you will find five internal waves within that leg. Once Wave C completes, we can expect prices to continue in the direction of the overall trend which is down in this case.

Running flat

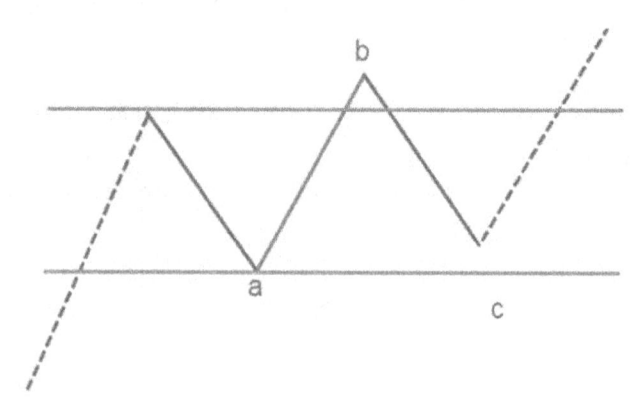

Figure 3-8: Running flat

42

The final type in the list is the ***running flat***. The running flat is the least common type of flat correction.

In a typical running flat, Wave B travels to a new extreme, exceeding the starting point of Wave A. However, unlike an expanding flat, Wave C in a running flat fails to reach the termination point of Wave A. Essentially, in an uptrend, Wave C will have a higher low than Wave A, and in a downtrend, Wave C will have a lower high than Wave A.

What does this tell us? We can say the market is highly energized and is ready to take off.

The problem with running flats is that in many cases, what appears to be a running flat often results in the formation of an expanding flat. Once a running flat is confirmed, it provides a strong signal of a healthy trend in progress.

Let's see what a running flat looks like on a price chart.

Figure 3-9: Running flat pattern

In this example, you will see that Wave B extends beyond Wave A and then moves lower to form Wave C, which doesn't reach the low of Wave A. Again, as I've mentioned, a running flat is difficult to recognize as completed in real-time, and in fact, many patterns that resemble a running flat will eventually extend to form an expanding flat. You want to make sure that you're not jumping the gun and labeling a flat as a running variety prematurely. In this case, the price action has provided enough data for us to classify this as a running flat. Once Wave C is completed, we can expect prices to continue in the direction of the prevailing trend.

So, we've gone over every characteristic of three types of flat patterns. In the next section, we'll discover the last type of corrective pattern: ***the triangles***.

## Triangle patterns

Triangles are five-wave corrective patterns that move against the trend and are labeled A, B, C, D, and E. They have a sideways price movement which tends to prolong the correction phase. The volatility decreases dramatically during its formation as prices seem to be locked into a tight range.

Triangles can be classified as contracting or expanding. A contracting triangle, as the name suggests, contracts as it progresses. An expanding triangle, on the other hand, expands as it progresses. The contracting triangle is more common than the expanding triangle.

While there is only one type of expanding triangle, there are three types of contracting triangle formations that take on the corrective form, including the **symmetrical triangle**, the **ascending triangle**, and the **descending triangle**. Technically speaking, the ascending and descending triangles are classified as barrier triangles within the context of Elliott Wave rules. However, for the sake of simplicity and since they are essentially contracting in nature, I include them in the contracting variety.

Most triangles precede the last wave of a larger sequence. In other words, they indicate that there is only one final move left in the direction of the prevailing trend before a reversal occurs. For example, a corrective triangle often occurs in the Wave 4 position which precedes the final Wave 5 within the impulse phase. They can also be found regularly in the Wave B position preceding the final Wave B of the zigzag formation. Let's take a look at the internal structure of a triangle.

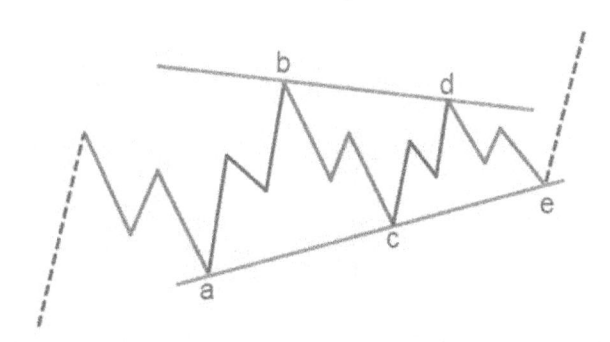

Figure 3-10: Triangle pattern

This substructure applies to all the different types of corrective triangle patterns that we will be discussing. Triangles have five waves labeled A, B, C, D, and E. Each of these waves subdivides into three smaller waves, hence triangles are considered 3-3-3-3-3 patterns. At least four of the waves within the triangle will be zigzag patterns. We can draw a trend line connecting Waves B and D on one side, and A and C on the other side. By doing so, we can see whether the triangle pattern is of a contracting variety or expanding variety. In this case, it's a contracting variety.

The B-D trend line within the triangle holds a special significance within the triangle structure, meaning that when the formation has completed its final E wave leg, a break of the B-D line within the triangle can offer a solid opportunity to trade the breakout.

Now, let's take a look at this diagram of the symmetrical triangle.

## Symmetrical triangle

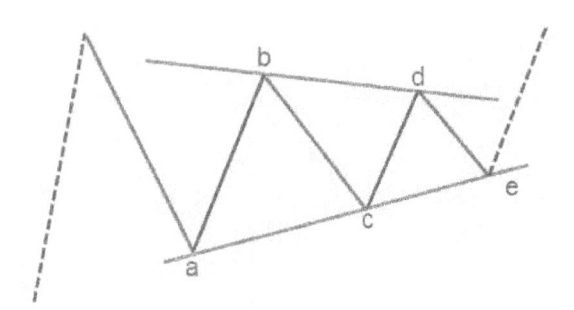

Figure 3-11: Symmetrical triangle

As you can see, the distinguishing characteristic of the **symmetrical triangle** is that it contracts from both sides and the waves become smaller as the pattern progresses. In the symmetrical triangle, each wave is shorter than the previous one, meaning that Wave B doesn't break the start of Wave A, Wave C doesn't break the starting point of Wave B, etc. Notice how these rules apply within this idealized structure. Also, remember that symmetrical triangles can occur in both uptrends and downtrends.

Now let's take a quick look at a symmetrical triangle on a price chart.

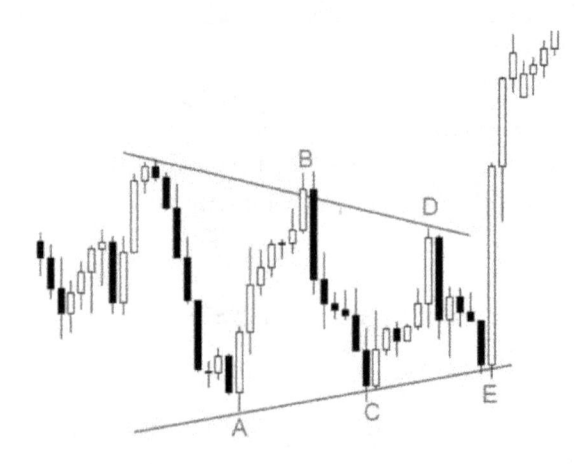

Figure 3-12: Symmetrical triangle

46

You can see the symmetrical triangle labeled A, B, C, D, and E, and its obvious contracting nature. Notice how the high of Wave D is lower than that of Wave B, the low of Wave C is higher than that of Wave A, and the low of Wave E is higher than that of Wave C. This example appears within a bull market, and we can expect the price to move higher after it completes Wave E and breaks the B-D trend line.

## Ascending triangle

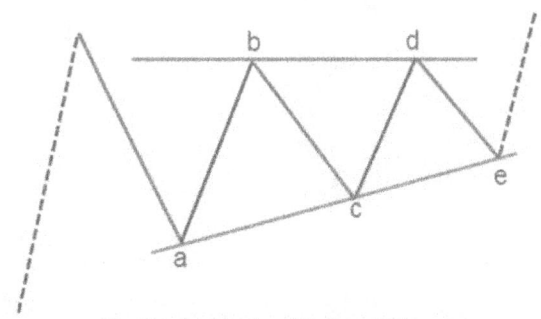

Figure 3-13: Ascending Triangle

Now, let's take a look at the **_ascending triangle_**. An ascending triangle has converging lines with a flat top and an upward sloping bottom. Essentially, the upper boundary forms a horizontal resistance line while the lower trend line rises progressively higher. This pattern indicates that the demand is building at the lows of Waves A, C, and E as the market is continually making higher lows. Ascending triangles occur predominantly in an uptrend. Take a look at the chart below.

Figure 3-14: Ascending triangle

Within this ascending triangle, the A-C trend line slopes upward while the B-D trend line is horizontal. The bulls are able to push to higher and higher lows that correspond to increasing demand. This increased demand contributes to the upward slope of the A-C trend line. We would expect the price to move higher after it completes Wave E and breaks the B-D trend line.

Descending triangle

Let's now look at the opposite of the ascending triangle: the **descending triangle**.

48

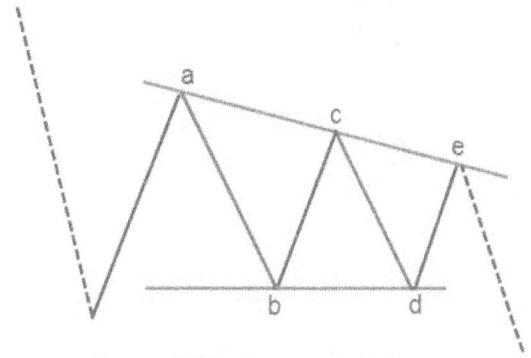

Figure 3-15: Descending triangle

A descending triangle has a converging formation with a flat bottom and a downward-sloping top. Essentially, the upper boundary forms a downward sloping trend line while the lower boundary is contained within a horizontal support line. The price action within a descending triangle pattern tells us that the supply or selling pressure is building at the highs of Waves A, C, and E as the market is continually making lower highs. Descending triangles occur predominantly in a downtrend.

Figure 3-16: Descending triangle

Within this descending triangle, the A-C trend line slopes downward while the B-D trend line is horizontal. The bears are able to push the price down to lower and lower highs that correspond to increasing supply. This increased supply causes the downward slope of the A-C trendline. We would expect the price to move lower after it completes Wave E and breaks the B-D trend line.

Expanding triangle

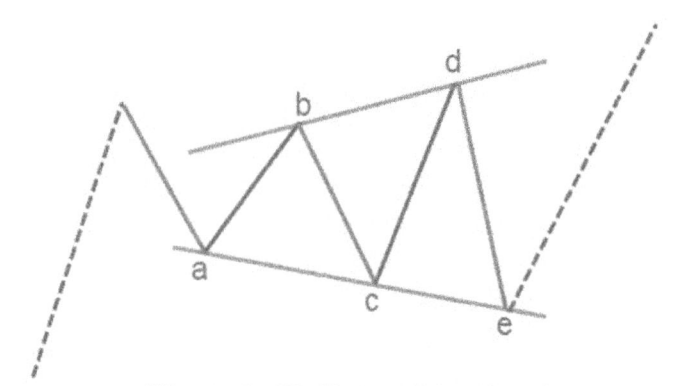

Figure 3-17: Expanding triangle

The final type of triangle pattern is the *expanding triangle*. It is also referred to as a reverse symmetrical triangle. Expanding triangles can occur in both uptrends and downtrends. As you can see from this illustration of an expanding triangle, the trend lines diverge as the waves progress. As a result, the overall range expands. This type of structure is the trickiest one to breakout traders since they inherently lead to false breakout scenarios.

Figure 3-18: Expanding triangle

This is an example of an expanding triangle on a price chart. Notice how the A-C trend line slopes upward and the B-D trend line slopes downward, creating an expanding range as the triangle progresses. Expanding triangles are quite rare, hence we don't expect to see them so often. In any case, when they form, a great entry location often exists just short of the A-C trend line where Wave E is likely to complete.

Running triangle

Now that we've looked at the various types of triangle structures, I want to go over a variation that can occur among all of these triangle structures: the ***running triangle***.

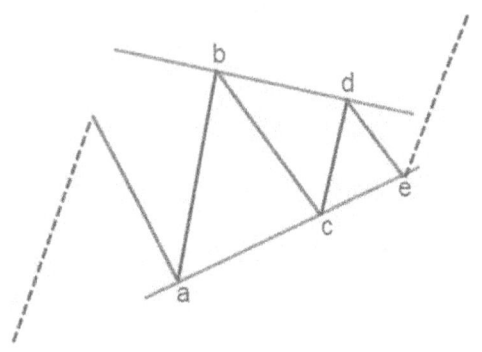

Figure 3-19: Running triangle

This image depicts a symmetrical triangle, but can you notice something different about this formation? Let's look closely at the start of Wave A of the triangle and where Wave B terminates in relation to the start of Wave A. Can you see that Wave B extends beyond the start of Wave A?

When this occurs, we refer to the triangle as a running triangle. Essentially, we have a running symmetrical triangle. Running triangles do occur quite frequently, hence it's important to be on the lookout for this variation. By doing so, we can better ensure that the wave labeling is done correctly.

Now, let's see what a running triangle looks like on an actual price chart.

Figure 3-20: Running triangle

On this chart, we can see how Wave B extends beyond the start of Wave A. Obviously, the Wave B labeling would be difficult to do at the time Wave B was unfolding, but you still need to keep that possibility open in your mind. As a triangle formation progressed further, it became increasingly apparent that the structure was likely a running triangle variation. Also, notice how nicely each of the sub-waves divides into three waves that resemble zigzag patterns.

The presence of the running triangle doesn't often change how we ultimately trade the pattern, but being aware that it does exist will greatly assist us in labeling waves correctly.

## **Combinations**

As of now, we've discussed the three types of simple corrective patterns: zigzags, flats, and triangles. In addition, we've gone over the different variations of each. Now, we'll take it one step further by learning how these single corrective structures combine to form combination patterns. More specifically, a ***corrective combination*** occurs when two or three corrective patterns combine to form a larger corrective structure.

As we've noted in our earlier discussion of single corrective patterns, there are two types of price movements: sharp and sideways corrections. The same concept can be applied to corrective combinations. You may recall that a zigzag is considered a sharp correction while flats and triangles belong to the sideways variety.

Zigzags can combine to form a larger structure. When two zigzags combine to form a larger structure, it's often called a double zigzag. When three zigzags combine together, it's referred to as a triple zigzag. A triple zigzag will be the limit, meaning that any zigzag combination will not include more than three zigzags. Double zigzags are much more prevalent than triple zigzags.

The second category of combinations includes double threes and triple threes which tend to have a sideways price action. A double three is a sideways combination of two corrective patterns while a triple three is a combination of three corrective patterns. As with the triple zigzag, a triple combination will be the limit, meaning that any structure will not combine more than three patterns. Also, double threes are much more common than triple threes.

## Double Zigzag

Let's take a look at the ***double zigzag*** pattern.

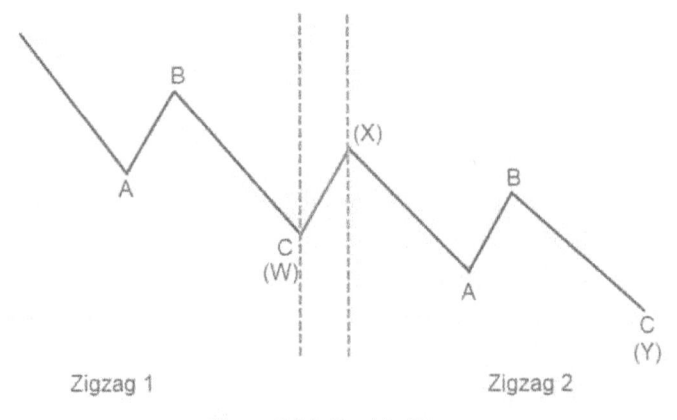

Figure 3-21: Double Zigzag

A double zigzag moves sharply against the trend and consists of two zigzag patterns. In both zigzags above, the sub-waves are denoted with the letters A, B, and C. The first zigzag pattern is labeled (W) while the second one is labeled (Y). The intervening wave which links the two is labeled (X). Hence, the double zigzag pattern forms a (W)-(X)-(Y) structure. Double zigzags tend to occur when the first zigzag does not make an adequate retracement to the trend, thus a doubling is often required to mark a sufficient price retracement. Let's have a look at a double zigzag on a price chart.

Figure 3-22: Double zigzag pattern

On this chart, we have an uptrend in place and a double zigzag pattern that corrects the previous leg. We can see that the first zigzag is labeled (W), the second zigzag is labeled (Y), and the connecting wave is labeled (X). As expected, the double zigzag makes a sharp correction, and then the price resumes in the direction of the overall trend.

Note: Wave (X) could be any corrective pattern but tend to be a zigzag.

Triple Zigzag

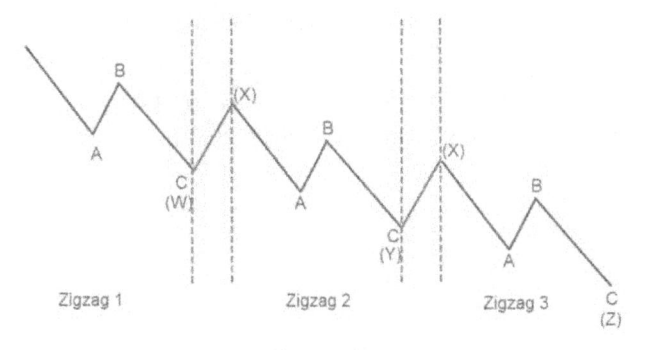

Figure 3-23: Triple Zigzag

55

Now, let's turn our attention to this illustration which depicts the ***triple zigzag*** pattern. The triple zigzag moves sharply against the trend and consists of three zigzag patterns. As with the double zigzag formation, the first zigzag within the overall structure is labeled (W) and the second one is labeled (Y). Since we have an additional zigzag within the structure, we would also need to label this with the letter (Z). There are two intervening waves that link the three zigzag patterns labeled as (X), giving the overall structure a naming convention of (W)-(X)-(Y)-(X)-(Z). Triple zigzags are not so common. As with double zigzags, they tend to occur when the first zigzag does not make an adequate retracement of the prior leg. Below is a real price chart that formed a triple zigzag pattern.

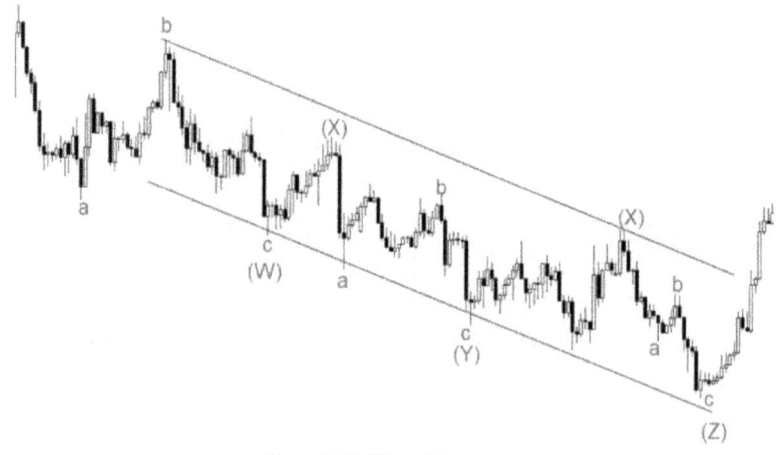

Figure 3-24: Triple zigzag pattern

In this example, we have three zigzags labeled as (W), (Y), and (Z). The two connecting waves that join the three are labeled (X). One characteristic of double and triple zigzags is that they tend to trade within well-defined channel lines and the price action tends to overlap. When you have a prolonged move that has both of these features, it is more likely that the structure is a double or triple zigzag.

## Double three and triple three

Now, let's discuss the double three and triple three combinations. The double three and triple three extend the duration of the price action during the correction. The naming convention is the same for double threes as they are with double zigzags and the same for triple threes as they are with triple zigzags. More specifically, a double three is labeled (W)-(X)-(Y) while a triple three is labeled (W)-(X)-(Y)-(X)-(Z).

Typically, in the double and triple three combinations, the initial wave will be the deepest retracement in terms of price. The other components of the corrective structure seem to widen the length of the correction without making a considerable price retracement. Volatility tends to become depressed during these times, making trading very difficult, especially for the not-so-patient traders. Therefore, it's best to remain on the sidelines during its progression.

Having said that, keep in mind that no retracement lasts forever, which is the reason we should be aware of the possibility of a double or triple three. Recognizing these combination patterns on the chart put us in a better position for trading the next impulse move after the correction completes.

## Double three

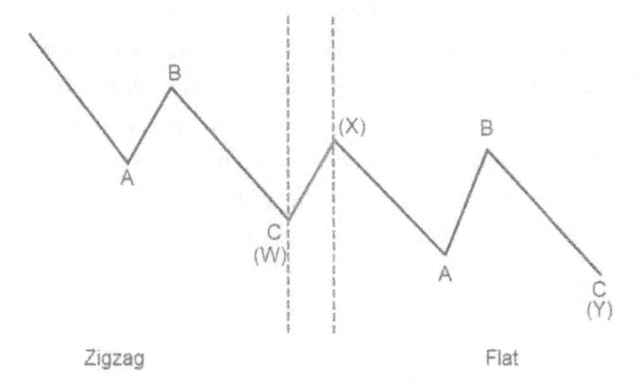

Figure 3-25: Zigzag - Flat

In this diagram, we can see what a ***double-three*** combination looks like. This variation consists of ***a zigzag and a flat***. The first part of this structure is a zigzag and is labeled (W). The sub-waves of Wave (W) are labeled A, B, and C. The second part of the structure is a flat - a regular flat. We have labeled the flat with the letter (Y), and you will note the internal waves labeled A, B, and C. The intervening wave that links the zigzag and the flat is upward in this case and is labeled (X).

Let's move on to some other variations of a double three.

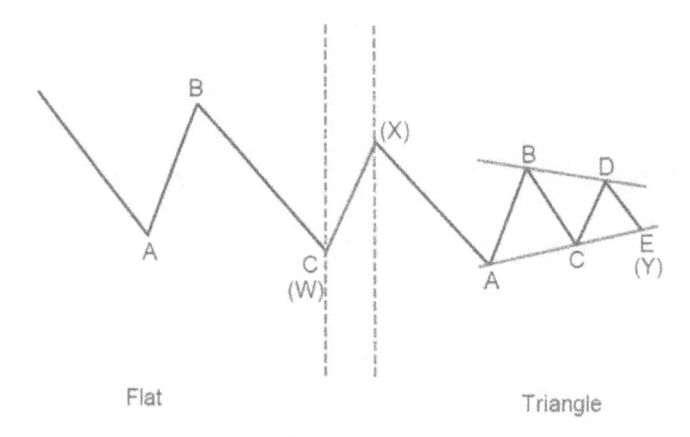

Figure 3-26: Flat - Triangle

We can see the ***flat-triangle*** combination in this figure. The initial corrective pattern is a regular flat which is labeled (W). The sub-waves of Wave (W) are labeled A, B, and C. The second corrective pattern is a symmetrical triangle. We've labeled the triangle with the letter (Y), and you will see the sub-waves of the triangle labeled A, B, C, D, and E. The connecting wave that links the flat with the triangle is labeled (X). It's important to note that when a triangle exists within a sideways combination, it would typically be the last corrective pattern. In addition, there can only be one triangle within the combination.

Let's move to another type of a double three.

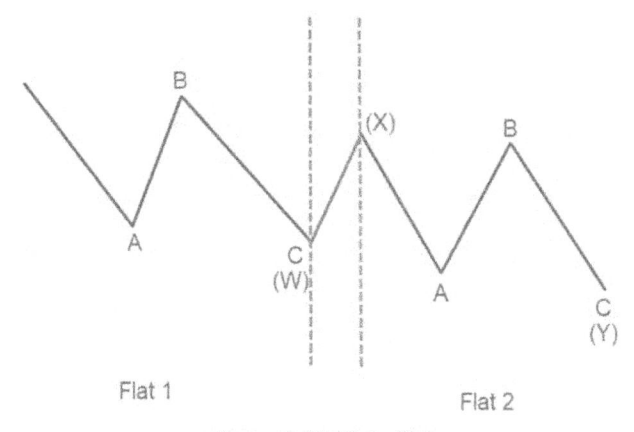

Figure 3-27: Flat - Flat

This example shows the **flat-flat** combination. Both corrective patterns within this double three are flats. The first flat is labeled (W) and the second one is labeled (Y). The sub-waves within the flat patterns are labeled A, B, and C. The intervening wave is labeled (X).

Triple Three

We've known some of the variations that double threes can take, but what about **triple threes**? What are some forms that triple threes can take? Now, let's take a look at a few formations, starting with a triple three combination that consists of *a zigzag, a flat, and a triangle.*

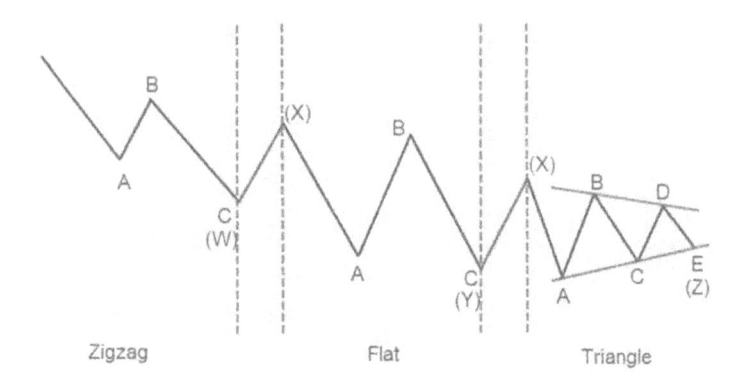

Figure 3-28: Zigzag - Flat - Triangle

If you look closely at the diagram above, you will see three corrective patterns: the first is a zigzag, the second is a flat, and the third is a triangle. The three corrective patterns are labeled (W), (Y) and (Z) respectively while the two waves that link the corrective patterns are labeled (X).

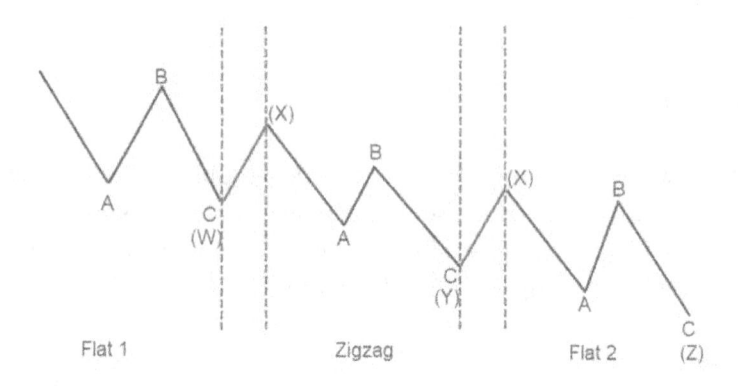

Figure 3-29: Flat - Zigzag - Flat

In this illustration, we have the *flat-zigzag-flat* combination. The first and third corrective patterns are flats, and the second is a zigzag. These patterns are labeled (W), (Y), and (Z) respectively, and (X) is the connecting wave. Within the context of triple threes, it's important to note that there can be no more than one zigzag.

Finally, let's take a look at the **flat-flat-flat** combination in the diagram below.

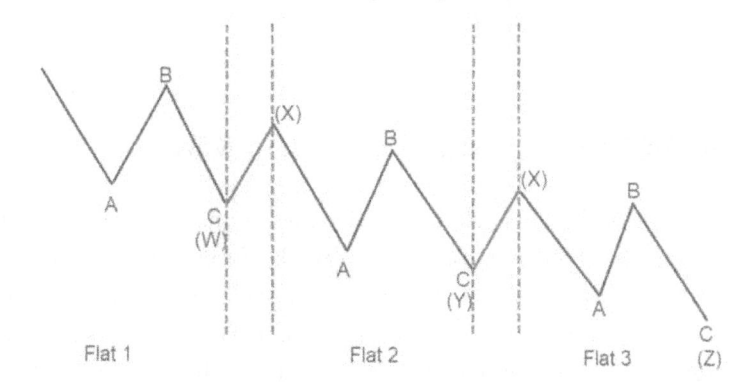

Figure 3-30: Flat - Flat - Flat

As the name suggests, this structure consists of three flats. More specifically, all three patterns fall into the regular flat variation. These three corrective flat patterns are labeled (W), (Y), and (Z) respectively, and the two waves that link the three flats are labeled (X).

That concludes this chapter about corrective waves. We've discovered a lot of knowledge about the three types of corrective patterns, and the different combinations between them. I know that it's difficult to absorb all of them at once. But don't worry, you'll get familiar with them with a certain amount of practice with real charts. In the next chapter, we'll focus on useful guidelines and channeling techniques that will greatly assist us in executing our trading strategies with the Elliott Wave principle.

# CHAPTER 4: ELLIOTT WAVE GUIDELINES & CHANNELING TECHNIQUES

## Guideline of Alternation and The Depth of Waves

We briefly discussed the guideline of alternation in one of the earlier sections. In this section, we will dive into the concept a bit further. Also, we'll discover the guideline for the depth of waves and the channeling techniques in the context of Elliott Wave trading. But first, it's important to understand that the guideline of alternation is not a hard and fast rule. It has a tendency to occur but is not a requirement that needs to be met.

Guideline of Alternation

Essentially, the guideline of alternation states that within the five-wave impulse sequence, Waves 2 and 4 will often alternate in form. Specifically, if Wave 2 is a simple sharp correction, Wave 4 will most likely be a simple sideways correction or complex sideways correction, and vice versa. In most cases, Wave 2 is a simple zigzag pattern and Wave 4 is a simple sideways correction. Although this guideline doesn't tell us the exact corrective pattern, we should expect to use the information from Wave 2 to exclude certain possibilities for Wave 4.

Let's take a look at the illustration below so that we can visualize this concept a little better.

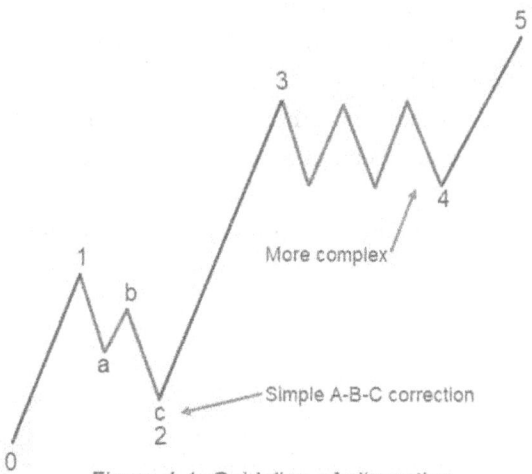

Figure 4-1: Guideline of alternation

In this example, notice how Wave 2 is a simple sharp correction while Wave 4 is a sideways correction. This fulfills the guideline of alternation where Waves 2 and 4 have different types of corrective price movement.

Another possibility is that Wave 2 is more complex while Wave 4 is a simple sharp correction. This also serves to fulfill the guideline of alternation. However, this scenario is generally uncommon in the financial markets. If you're wondering why, it's just about the psychology of market participants at Wave 2 versus Wave 4. During Wave 2, traders are expecting continued pressure in the direction of the prior trend, which results in a deep retracement. Meanwhile, Wave 4 is associated more with profit-taking, therefore the correction tends to be prolonged and shallow.

Guideline on the depth of waves

Next, let's discuss another important guideline called the depth of corrective waves.

What does this guideline tell us?

The depth of corrective waves states that when the market is in a correction, it will often retrace to the price territory of the *previous fourth wave of a smaller degree*. Keep in mind that for this guideline, we are not talking about a specific point on the chart, but rather an area of interest. The market often finds support or resistance around this zone before the trend resumes.

Let's move to a visual illustration of this guideline for a better understanding.

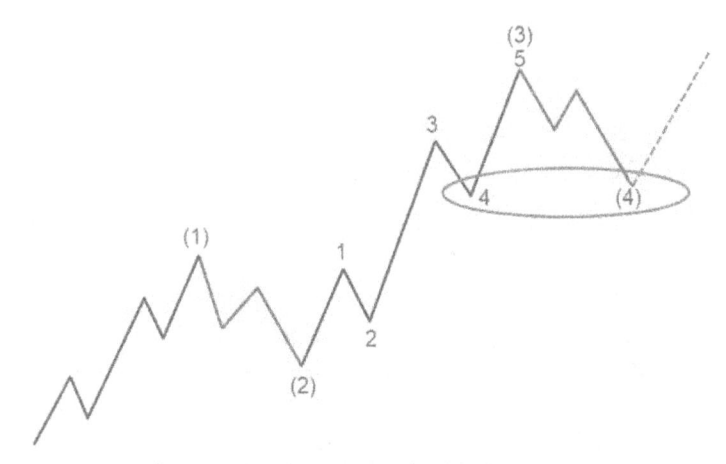

Figure 4-2: The depth of waves

In this illustration, you can see Waves (1) through (4) of the intermediate degree. The smaller degree waves are noted within the impulse Wave (3). You can see Wave (4) ends within the span of wave 4 of the smaller degree, which is circled on the chart. This guideline is most useful when the larger degree wave under consideration is the fourth wave itself.

Now that we've gone over the guideline of alternation and the guideline of the depth of corrective waves, it's now time to move on to one of my favorite applications in Elliott Wave trading: the *channeling technique*.

## Channeling techniques

One of the most practical applications within the framework of Elliott Wave analysis is the use of price channels. Essentially, an Elliott Wave price channel

64

is comprised of two parallel lines. Price action will often move within these parallel channels and at the same time marks the upper and lower boundaries of the channels. Therefore, these parallel channels should be drawn at specific stages during the price development to gain insights into the probable termination point for the current wave under consideration. However, unlike price channels that many other technical analysts draw on the chart in a seemingly random fashion, Elliot Wave channels provide well-defined rules that guide the construction of the proper parallel channel at every stage of the 5-3 structure.

There are **five types of price channels** that we should be aware of. The channeling technique applied to each of these is the same, however, their names are derived from their position within the overall cycle. Additionally, there are different implications for each of these as we will see shortly. Also, we should note that the names of each type of price channel vary a bit from Elliott's original terminology. I have adopted the terminology used by Jeffrey Kennedy since I believe that these terms are more appropriate and specific to the analysis of the current wave progression under consideration.

The five types of channels in Elliott Wave theory include:

- Base channel: To confirm Wave 3 price action.
- Acceleration channel: To find the end of Wave 4.
- Deceleration channel: To provide a timely entry into Wave 5.
- Termination channel: To project the end of Wave 5.
- Corrective channel: To find the end of the 5-3 structure.

Now, let's discover each of these important price channels.

## Base channel

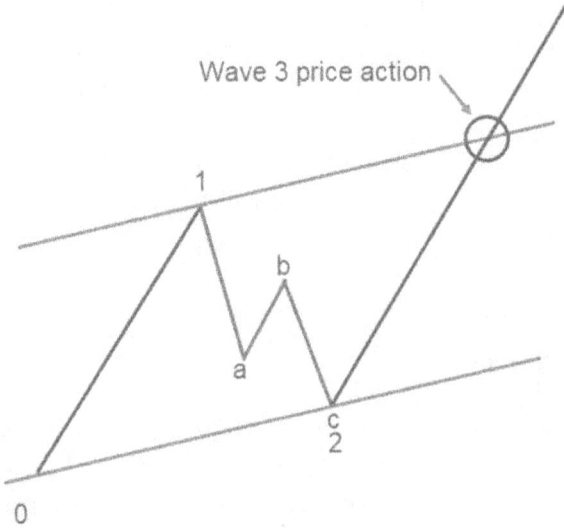

Figure 4-3: Base channel

A *base channel* can be drawn once Wave 2 has been completed. It requires three reference points: the start of Wave 1, the end of Wave 1, and the end of Wave 2. If you take a close look at this illustration, you'll find these three reference points labeled 0, 1, and 2 respectively. To draw the base channel, you would first draw a trend line from the start of Wave 1 to the end of Wave 2. After that, you would then construct a parallel trend line and place it on the extreme of Wave 1, creating the base channel. The primary purpose of the base channel is to confirm Wave 3 price action. In other words, if the price action penetrates the parallel line drawn from the end of Wave 1, this would be characteristic of Wave 3 price action. If, however, it rejects or bounces off that level in the opposite direction, there's a higher likelihood that the wave labeling may be incorrect, and what we may be looking at is a corrective structure rather than an impulsive one. Let's see what this looks like on a price chart.

Figure 4-4: Base channel

Once the second wave has finished, we can trace the base of the channel (the higher line) by connecting the start of Wave 1 to the end of Wave 2. After that, we trace the lower line of the channel starting at the end of Wave 1. We would wait to see how the price reacts at the lower parallel line. In this case, the price broke this line quite easily. This confirms that we are most likely seeing a Wave 3 in progress because Wave 3 is often the strongest wave with the steepest slope within the impulse sequence.

Acceleration channel

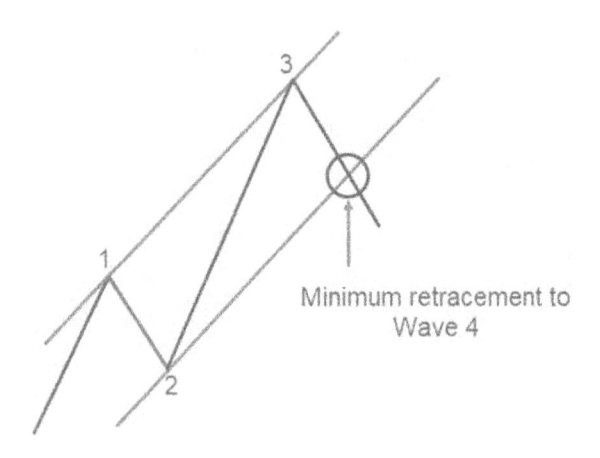

Figure 4-5: Acceleration channel

Now let's discuss the second type of price channel: the **trend channel**, or the **acceleration channel**. An acceleration channel can be drawn once Waves 1, 2, and 3 have been completed. It requires three reference points: the end of Wave 1, the end of Wave 2, and the end of Wave 3. To draw the acceleration channel, you would first need to draw a trend line from the end of Wave 1 to the end of Wave 3. Keep in mind that during the progression of Wave 3, it is quite common to redraw this line a few times as price makes continued progress in the direction of Wave 3. However, at some point, it will become clear that Wave 3 has ended and the placement of the 1-3 trend line can be finalized. Once the 1-3 trend line has been drawn, you would then construct its parallel trend line from the end of Wave 2, creating the acceleration channel. The acceleration channel can provide us with clues about the possible termination point for Wave 4. Typically, the lower parallel line will be the minimum target in both price and time for the Wave 4 completion. The acceleration channel requires us to be patient and wait when the price action falls short of the minimum price target for Wave 4.

One question can emerge as to whether this trendline is **always** the minimum price target for Wave 4? The answer is "No". It won't. However, in trading, we are only working with probabilities, and the scenario mentioned will hold in a large percentage of cases, especially when Wave 2 is a simple, sharp zigzag correction.

Figure 4-6: Acceleration channel

On this chart, we've drawn an acceleration channel. We would expect the minimum price and time projection for the end of Wave 4 to occur when the price action touches the lower parallel line. In this example, the price slightly touched the lower end of the acceleration channel and completed the Wave 4 correction before advancing into the final Wave 5. In many cases, when the corrective pattern in Wave 4 is a simple zigzag or flat, the price action may merely touch the parallel line and then move along its path. But in other cases, especially when a triangle or combination is in the works, the price action may often move beyond the boundary of the acceleration channel. When this happens, we can be on alert and expect the possibility of a prolonged correction phase.

Deceleration channel

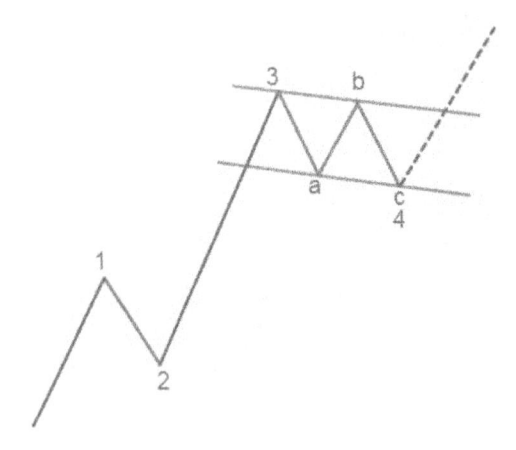

Figure 4-7: Deceleration channel

The next type of parallel channel is called the **deceleration channel**. A deceleration channel can be drawn once Wave 3 and sub-waves A and B of Wave 4 have been completed. To draw the deceleration channel, you would first need to draw a trend line from the end of Wave 3 to the end of Wave B. After that, you would take the parallel of this trend line and run it from the extreme of Wave A, creating the deceleration price channel. The deceleration channel will typically act to contain the corrective price action within Wave 4.

You should know by now that the fourth waves tend to carve out a sideways price action that can often be prolonged in nature. As a result, it can be quite challenging at times to accurately label the sub-waves within it the fourth wave. The deceleration channel can assist us in these circumstances when a clear count is not evident. When you're not able to definitively pinpoint Wave A and B within Wave 4, drawing the deceleration channel can be of great use. Once the price breaks out of the deceleration channel in a decisive manner and in the direction of the overall trend, we can be fairly confident that the Wave 4 corrective structure has ended and the Wave 5 impulse is underway. Below is a real price chart with a deceleration channel.

Figure 4-8: Deceleration channel

In this example, we can see that an uptrend has been in progress. The deceleration channel is drawn by connecting the end of Wave 3 to the end of sub-wave B and then tracing a parallel line starting at the end of sub-wave A. With the deceleration channel drawn, we would wait for the price to break decisively from this channel in the direction of the trend which is up in this case. If you take a close look at the price action at the breakout point, you'll notice the strong breakout candle that extends and closes beyond the upper end of the deceleration channel. This is a strong indication that Wave 4 is probably over and Wave 5 is in progress.

Termination channel

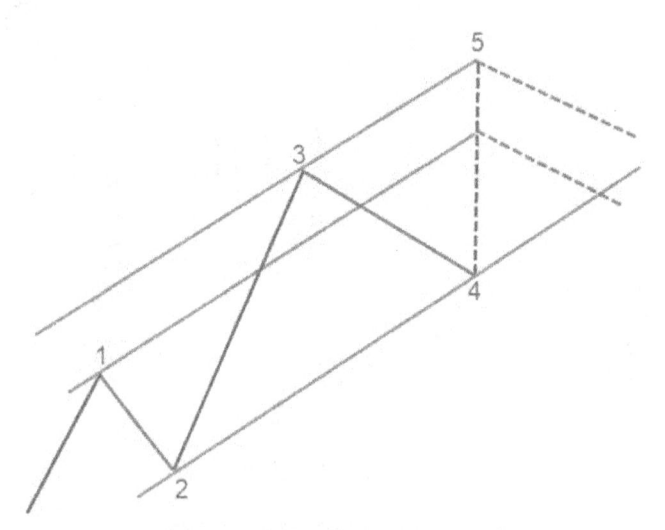

Figure 4-9: Termination channel

The next type of price channel is the **termination channel**. The termination channel helps us to pinpoint the end of Wave 5 within the impulse sequence. It can be drawn once Waves 2, 3, and 4 have been completed. To create the termination channel, you would begin by drawing a trend line from the end of Wave 2 to the end of Wave 4. After that, you would take a parallel of this trend line and run it from the end of Wave 3. If, however, the slope of the Wave 3 price action is very steep, it becomes more effective to run the parallel trend line off the end of Wave 1. If you're in doubt as to which of the two lines would work better, then plotting both and watching the price interaction around each area would be a viable option.

One important phenomenon that tends to occur in termination channels is something called a ***throwover***. A throwover is a scenario where the price penetrates the parallel trend line, but then quickly moves back within the channel. This indicates that the market is making one last push before impeding a trend change. Let's take a look at a termination channel drawn on a price chart.

Figure 4-10: Termination channel

The termination channel is drawn by first marking the trend line from the end of Wave 2 to the end of Wave 4, and then placing two parallel trend lines at the end of Wave 3 and Wave 1. Now, as Wave 5 progresses, we would expect price reaction at either of these trend lines as a possible termination point. Referring to the lower right side of this chart, you can see that the price penetrated the trend line drawn from the end of Wave 1 in what appears to be a throwover, and then quickly move back within the channel. As such, if you were in a short position, this would be an opportune time to exit. In addition, we would consider long opportunities because the weight of evidence is now starting to point to a possible trend change.

Corrective channel

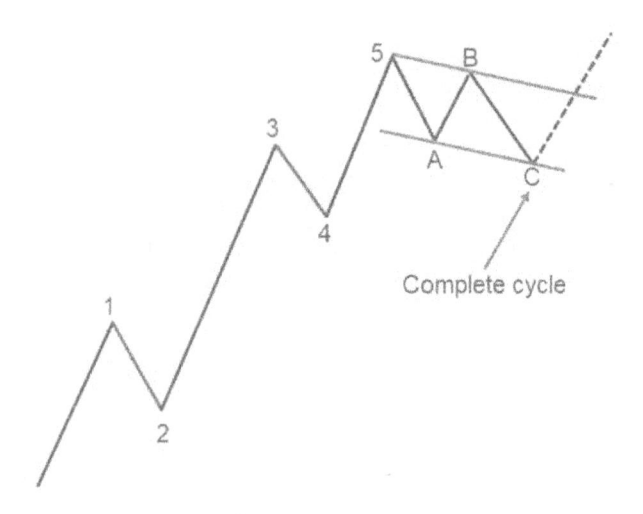

Figure 4-11: Corrective channel

The last price channel variation in the list is the *corrective channel*. It is similar to the deceleration channel that we discussed a bit earlier. However, as the name implies, it applies to the corrective phase of the 5-3 sequence. A corrective channel can be drawn once Wave 5, Wave A, and Wave B of the corrective sequence have been completed. You would first need to draw a trend line from the end of Wave 5 to the end of Wave B. After that, you would then take the parallel of this line and project it at the extreme of Wave A. There are two areas to watch closely within the corrective channel. The first one is the development of Wave C. Typically, during the Wave C progression, as price approaches the lower parallel trend line, we would expect a slowing of momentum as compared to Wave A. In many cases, this waning momentum will register as a momentum divergence and signals that the corrective sequence may be close to its termination point. The second scenario of interest will be the breakout of the 5-B trendline. Once the price breaks out of this trendline, we can be fairly confident that the corrective phase has ended, and we are in the early stages of the next impulse sequence. Let's turn our attention to the following price chart.

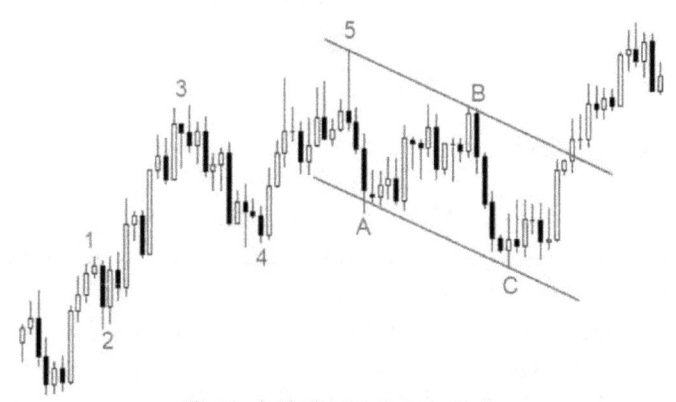

Figure 4-12: Corrective channel

We can see that the market is in an overall uptrend and the upward five-wave impulse sequence has formed. Along with its corresponding A-B-C corrective phase, the corrective channel would be drawn once Wave 5, Wave A, and Wave B have been completed. First, we would plot a trend line connecting the end of Wave 5 to the end of Wave B. Then, we would run a parallel line at the extreme of Wave A. Once the price breaks the upper channel boundary, we can be fairly confident that the uptrend is resuming and that a new five-wave impulse sequence to the upside is in the early stages.

The Elliott Wave channeling technique is one of my favorite methods for analyzing price action. I use it at virtually every stage within the 5-3 sequence. It's extremely powerful and something I would urge you to practice and implement regularly.

In the next chapter, we're going to start taking a deep dive into Fibonacci analysis and see how it's intertwined with Elliott Wave. You will understand how Elliott Wave cannot be used effectively without the help of powerful Fibonacci analysis.

# CHAPTER 5: FIBONACCI FOUNDATIONS

## Fibonacci Sequence

One of the most talented Western mathematician of the Middle Ages is Leonardo Pisano Bigollo, also referred to as Fibonacci. He was born in Pisa, Italy in the 12th century. Fibonacci was the son of a wealthy merchant. As a youngster, he traveled throughout North Africa with his father. During that period, he picked up and learned about ancient Hindu Arabic mathematics, and helped to popularize this knowledge in Europe, mainly through his writings.

Essentially, the Hindu Arabic numerals are a set of ten symbols - zero through nine - that represent numbers in the decimal-based system. In 1202, he published his famous book titled Liber Abaci, which stemmed from a two-year study of the pyramids of Giza. In this book, he advanced the idea of the Hindu Arabic numeral system. He believed it was superior to the traditional Roman numeral system that was currently in use at that time in Europe, but it took several centuries after its publication for the new system to become mainstream within Europe.

Fibonacci is recognized for the discovery of a particular sequence of numbers that is aptly named after him. Interestingly, the series was the answer to the question of how many rabbits can be produced in a year from the first two rabbits placed in a closed area.

So, what is this Fibonacci sequence? Essentially, the Fibonacci series takes 0 and 1 as the first two numbers, and each successive number within the sequence is the sum of the prior two adjacent ones as illustrated below.

0, 1, 1, 2, 3, 5, 8, 13, 21, 34, 55, 89, 144, 233, 377…

There are many characteristics that are unique to the Fibonacci sequence and are often referred to as nature's secret code. There are countless examples of the Fibonacci numbers present in the natural universe, from trees to planetary systems, and even our own DNA.

*First*, as you divide any Fibonacci number by its previous number, the resulting number approaches Phi or the golden ratio, approximately 1.618. Phi is an irrational number but is often rounded off to 1.618. The bigger the pair of Fibonacci numbers is, the closer the result approaches 1.618. Let's take a look at a few examples.

13 divided by 8 equals 1.625,

21 divided by 13 equals 1.615,

34 divided by 21 equals 1.619,

55 divided by 34 equals 1.618,

89 divided by 55 equals 1.618, and so on.

This ratio is seen in many ancient architectural sites, including the great pyramids of Giza. The ratio of each base to the height of the pyramid is a very close approximation to the golden ratio of 1.618. Nature also boasts many instances of the golden ratio. The bodies of animals, fingers, tree branches, and flower petals are just a few examples of the golden ratio seen in the natural world.

*Second*, as you divide any Fibonacci number by its following number, the resulting number approaches 0.618. The approximation nears 0.618 as the numbers increase. For example:

8 divided 13 equals 0.615,

13 divided by 21 equals 0.619,

21 divided by 34 equals 0.618,

34 divided by 55 equals 0.618, and so on.

Note: When it comes to the financial markets, 0.618 is one of the most significant if not the single most important Fibonacci ratios that traders should be aware of.

***Third***, as you divide any Fibonacci number by its second and third ladder number, the resulting numbers approach 0.382 and 0.236 respectively, and the approximations near those values as the numbers increase.

Along with other aspects of the natural universe, the markets also conform to various Fibonacci relationships. The reason for this lies in the reflection of mass human psychology, which is influenced by the universal laws of nature.

The waves within the market structure exhibit certain Fibonacci ratios and relationships among them. Fibonacci analysis works hand in hand with Elliott Wave. Elliott Wave helps to determine the structure within the price action while Fibonacci helps to set price objectives for the impulsive and corrective formations. They are complementary in nature and should be viewed as part of a cohesive whole.

There are four primary Fibonacci tools in the trading context: **Fibonacci retracements**, **Fibonacci extensions**, **Fibonacci projections**, and **Fibonacci time ratios**. In the next sections, we'll go over each of the Fibonacci tools that we will rely on in Elliott Wave Trading.

## Fibonacci Retracements

The Fibonacci retracement tool is a widely used tool among technical traders. It measures internal retracements within a price move. It is drawn by taking two extreme points - a major swing high and a major swing low. The retracement tool divides the area between the two selected points by the designated Fibonacci ratios, typically including the 23.6 percent, 38.2 percent, 50 percent, 61.8 percent, and 78.6 percent retracement levels. These levels represent hidden support and resistance in the market. Traders can use Fibonacci retracement levels as a way to find high probability entries and to place logical stop-loss orders.

Note: The 50 percent and 78.6 percent levels are not derived from the Fibonacci sequence, however, they are considered key Fibonacci retracement levels. The 50 percent level marks half of the price correction, hence triggering certain psychological reactions among traders. On the other hand, the 78.6 percent is the square root of 0.618, and adding this level to the list brings about a sense of balance, with the 50 percent level in the middle, two levels above, and two levels below.

As with all Fibonacci-based tools, determining which retracement levels to pay the most attention to depends on several factors. The most important of which is the current wave structure. Many times, when we use the Fibonacci retracement tool, we are selecting the start and the end of an impulse as two reference points. From there, we try to anticipate the likely extent of the pullback during the correction phase.

The 23.6 percent level is the shallowest retracement and can be seen during strongly trending markets such as in extensions within the Wave 3 position. The 38.2 percent level is a more common type of retracement level and occurs during normal trending conditions. Many Wave-4 corrections adhere to the 38.2 percent retracement level. As with the 50 percent retracement, as I mentioned, there is often a psychological effect that traders act upon when the price action retraces half the previous price move. The 61.8 percent retracement level is the most common within the markets which is frequently respected during a Wave-2 zigzag progression and is evident in many triangle patterns. The 78.6 percent retracement is fairly deep and also occurs frequently in the Wave-2 position, especially after a prolonged price move.

Figure 5-1: Fibonacci retracement

On this chart, we've plotted the Fibonacci retracement levels using the swing high on the upper left of the chart and the swing low on the lower portion of the chart. First, notice how the price reacts as it touches the 38.2 percent retracement level in the early stage of the retracement. Next, look at how the price stalls and bounces from the 61.8 percent and 78.6 percent levels as it approached these deep retracement areas. Obviously, not every retracement level would see a price reaction. But as we'll learn later, once we know where we are in the wave count, we can better predict which Fibonacci levels or zones should be the most important to watch in terms of potential reversals.

## Fibonacci Extensions

The Fibonacci extension tool is somewhat misunderstood among traders. Unlike the retracement tool, the extension tool measures an external retracement that moves beyond the selected swing points. Just as with retracements, two swing points are needed to measure an extension. The most common extension levels include 127.2 percent, 161.8 percent, 200 percent, and 261.8 percent. Most times, when we are using the extension tool, we are looking to project how far an impulse wave is likely to move. As such, we would select the beginning and end of a correction as the start and end points. Fibonacci extensions are less used as compared to Fibonacci retracements, and the relationships between waves from the extension standpoint are less reliable than that within internal retracements. Having said that, they can provide us with some insights into the strength of a move and its probable termination point.

The 127.2 percent extension level is often used to calculate the end of impulse Wave 5. To do this, you would use the start and the end of Wave 4 to calculate the extension level. The end of Wave 5 will often occur at or near this 127.2 percent extension level. The 200 percent and 261.8 percent extension levels are useful in calculating the zone for the end of impulse Wave 3. To do this, you would typically use the start and the end of Wave 2 to calculate the levels. The area between these two extension levels often acts as the termination point for Wave 3. Let's now turn our attention to a real price chart.

Figure 5-2: Fibonacci extension

Notice we've drawn a Fibonacci extension from the swing low at the left of the chart to the swing high which is a bit higher. The upward-sloping dotted line shows these two selected points on the chart. You can see the overlapping price action which suggests that this structure is probably a corrective pattern, and we would anticipate an impulse move following this correction. The first extension is 127.2 percent level. Below that is the 161.8 percent level. Notice how the price stalled as it approached this level which played as both support and resistance several times. The third extension on the chart is the 200 percent level. Finally, we have the 261.8 percent extension level acting as a key support area before the price made a strong bounce back to the upside.

## Fibonacci Projections

Fibonacci projections, which are also referred to as Fibonacci expansions within some platforms, are another important Fibonacci application that is of great help in Elliott Wave trading. As you may recall from our earlier discussion on retracements and extensions, these tools only require two swing points to calculate respective levels. With the Fibonacci projection tool, we need three swing points in order to calculate its levels. That's one thing that sets it apart from the other two Fibonacci tools.

Basically, Fibonacci expansions are price levels that are created by selecting a price move from swing A to B and its corresponding retracement at swing C. Once these points are in place, the projection levels reflect the ratios of the distance from swing A to B measured from swing C. The most common Fibonacci projection levels include 61.8 percent, 100 percent, 127.2 percent, and 161.8 percent. With the projection tool, we try to gauge how far a particular wave (that is moving in the same direction as the one that we are measuring) is likely to travel. This tool is particularly useful when we want to find the probable termination points of Wave 3 of an impulse, Wave 5 of an impulse, and Wave C of a regular flat or zigzag correction. We can anticipate the length of Waves 3 and 5 by using a Fibonacci ratio of the length of Wave 1. As we will learn later, both Wave 3 and Wave 5 have specific Fibonacci relationships to Wave 1. Moreover, we can look for the probable termination point of Wave C by comparing its price move to the length of Wave A. We will be going over all of this in more detail in the upcoming sections, but for now, it's important to understand how to use the Fibonacci projection tool.

Looking at different expansion levels, the length of Wave 5 is often equal or 0.618 times the length of Wave 1. As such, the 61.8 percent and 100 percent projection levels are often used to determine the likely end of Wave 5 in comparison with Wave 1.

The length of Wave C is often equal to the length of Wave A, but sometimes approximates 127 percent of the length of Wave A. As such, the 100 percent and 127 percent projection levels are used regularly in projecting the end of Wave C in comparison with Wave A.

The length of Wave 3 is often 1.618 times the length of Wave 1. This is one of the strongest Fibonacci relationships between waves moving in the same direction. It's an extremely important relationship to keep in mind when determining the likely ending of Wave 3. For example, if the Wave 3 projection fails to reach approximately 161.8 percent of Wave 1, we may want to reassess our count and consider the possibility that the structure under consideration may actually be corrective rather than impulsive.

Figure 5-3: Fibonacci projection

In this example, you can see the Fibonacci projection levels plotted using the three swing points: A, B, and C. Do not confuse them with Waves A, B, and C. These swing points have nothing to do with wave count. They are merely used to help visualize the points in the construction of the Fibonacci projection levels.

Starting at the top of the chart, the first projection is the 61.8 percent level, which is just below the Swing B. After that, we have the 100 percent level which acts as support a few times. Just above that, you'll see the 127.2 percent level, and the last level is the 161.8 percent level. Notice after swing C completes, the price action moves up to the 161.8 percent level before bouncing back and consolidating in a range created by the 161.8 percent and 100 percent levels. You should be able to see the five-wave structure to the upside.

## Fibonacci Time Zones

The Fibonacci time ratio is the last Fibonacci tool we discuss. When most traders do their analysis, they're often making some sort of assumptions based on price, but rarely take time analysis into consideration.

What exactly is time analysis?

Simply put, just as the Fibonacci ratios can tell us the *price levels* that can likely lead to price reactions, time ratios can clue us into the *time levels* that price reactions may happen. A time level is simply a future time when a price reaction or turning point is likely to occur. Think of it as support and resistance based on time. One of the most powerful trading signals that you can get is when price and time align within a narrow window.

To plot the Fibonacci time ratio, we need two reference points: a swing high and a swing low. The Fibonacci time ratio will then plot as vertical lines extended into the future. The most important time ratios are 38.2 percent; 61.8 percent; 100 percent; and 161.8 percent.

Keep in mind that Fibonacci time ratios are not as reliable as the other Fibonacci tools that are based on price, but there are certain instances when the time ratios prove to be extremely valuable. The most important of which is when we are looking for the termination point of Wave 4. Simple Wave 4 corrections typically terminate between 61.8 percent and 100 percent of the time elapsed in the Wave 3 formation. Knowing this tendency will help prevent us from entering into a fifth wave prematurely.

The best way to apply Fibonacci time ratios is to treat them as zones rather than hard and fast points along the time series. Sharp Wave 2 corrections often take 38.2 percent to 61.8 percent of the time that Wave 1 does. Simple Wave 4 corrections often take 61.8 percent to 100 percent of the time that Wave 3 does.

Of these two tendencies, the second relationship is stronger. Let's see what this looks like on a price chart.

Figure 5-4: Fibonacci time zone

On this chart, I've selected the swing from low to high as you can see by the dashed line towards the center of the chart. Once these two reference points are selected, the Fibonacci time ratios are automatically plotted across the time axis in vertical lines. The first time ratio is the 38.2 percent ratio, followed by the 61.8 percent ratio. Notice how this retracement of the prior swing ended almost exactly at this golden level. Also, toward the right of the chart, we have the 100 percent and 161.8 percent time ratios plotted.

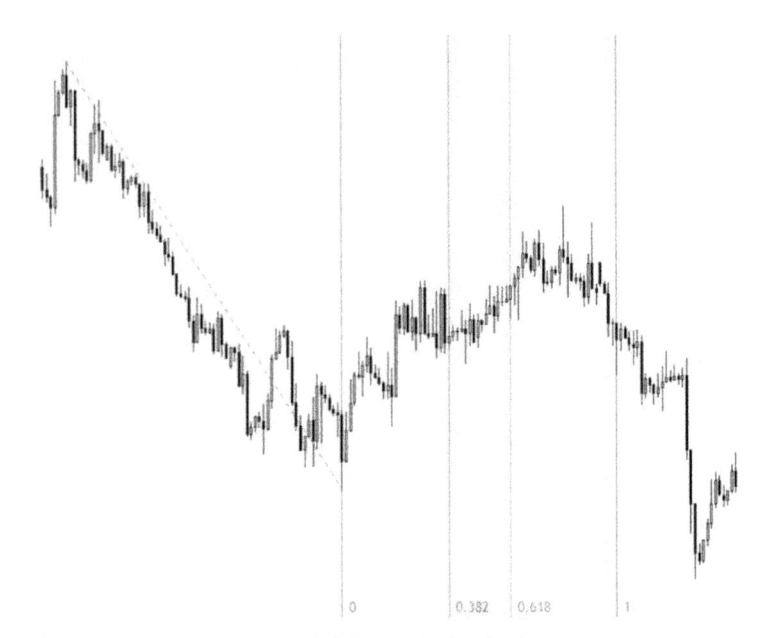

Figure 5-5: Fibonacci time zone

In this example, I've used the swing from high to low to calculate the 61.8 percent and 100 percent time projections. Can you see how the price retracement ends? Right in the middle of this zone before supply starts to pick up. The 61.8 percent - 100 percent Fibonacci time zone marks the end of the corrective move and soon afterward, prices rise to a new low. If we hadn't plotted this zone, we may have been tempted into taking a short position a bit earlier. Once these ratio lines have been plotted, we knew to wait as the correction was likely not yet completed from the time perspective. There are countless times when the Fibonacci time projection has saved me from entering a position prematurely.

This brings us to the end of the chapter. I hope you're getting comfortable with the different types of Fibonacci studies and how to apply them. Remember when analyzing time and price ratios for the purpose of finding potential turning points, you should always treat them as zones rather than single fixed points.

In the next two chapters, we're going to dig deeper into the art of combining Fibonacci ratios with the different waves within the overall cycle.

# CHAPTER 6: FIBONACCI AND THE IMPULSE PHASE

## Combining Elliott Wave And Fibonacci

Elliott Wave analysis goes hand in hand with Fibonacci analysis. Elliott Wave provides us with a framework from which we can analyze various price action structures within the market, and the application of Fibonacci-based tools helps us to identify high probability targets for the termination of waves within the overall structure.

There are many traders out there that consider themselves well-versed in Fibonacci analysis. However, without a proper understanding and cohesive implementation of it with the Elliott Wave principle, these traders are simply not getting the full benefit that can be derived from a more holistic approach that combines both. The mathematical fabric within the Elliott Wave patterns is linked to the Fibonacci sequence, specifically to the Fibonacci-derived ratios. Therefore, it is essential that the two are considered and treated as parts that make up a whole rather than mutually exclusive concepts. This is why you sometimes hear some traders complain that they've tried to use the concepts within Fibonacci but could not find any success with it. The problem is not with the concepts, but with the application of those concepts. This means that you cannot simply rely on price to react to each Fibonacci level arbitrarily, but instead, you need to have a clear idea of where you are within the overall wave structure. This will allow you to successfully apply the highest probability Fibonacci ratios for that particular wave cycle.

In this chapter, we will focus on relationships within the impulse phase. We'll take the concepts we learned about Elliott Wave and Fibonacci and merge them into a cohesive, more statistical-based method. I hope you're as excited about learning this as I am in presenting it to you.

# Fibonacci Ratios for Wave 2

Price relationship

Let's turn our attention to this illustration below:

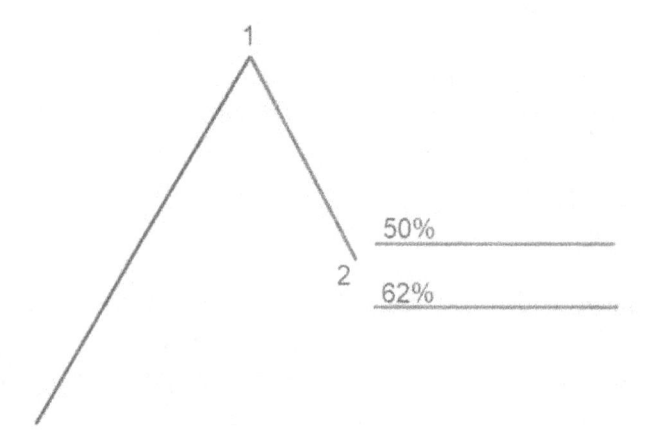

Figure 6-1: Fib ratios for Wave 2

In this illustration, the upward line represents an impulse move in Wave 1, and the downward line represents a retracement against Wave 1, which is Wave 2. We would use the Fibonacci retracement tool to measure the beginning of Wave 1 to the end of Wave 1. By selecting these two points, the chart will automatically draw your predefined Fibonacci levels. The most common Fibonacci retracement for Wave 2 is a 50 percent - 62 percent retracement of Wave 1.

Note: For the sake of simplicity, I will round off the decimal place when talking about Fibonacci ratios. For example, I often refer to the 61.8 percent ratio as 62 percent, and I'll do the same with many other ratios as well. It's just easier from the discussion standpoint and it doesn't materially change what we're talking about.

Again, Wave 2 retracement often ends between 50 percent and 62 percent of the length of Wave 1. Take a look at the price chart below.

Figure 6-2: 50% - 62% Fib retracement

On this chart, the price moves up in an impulsive manner, creating the Wave 1 high. Then, it begins to consolidate and move lower as it corrects the first wave. Among the retracement lines plotted by the Fibonacci retracement tool, notice the 50 percent and the 62 percent retracement levels. When the price reaches this zone, it consolidates within the two boundaries for quite some time before continuing with the overall trend. Starting from this strong consolidation area, the price easily takes out the Wave 1 high when it travels into Wave 3.

Figure 6-3: 50% - 62% Fib retracement

Here's another example of a Wave 2 retracement. The price starts with a strong move within Wave 1. Following that, it begins its upward retracement during the Wave 2 correction phase. As soon as the price interacts with the 50 percent level, the correction ends and prices begin to move lower into the impulse Wave 3. You should be able to see the 5-wave subdivision within Wave 3 which ends near the bottom right of the chart.

Time relationship

Now, let's move to the time relationship between the two waves.

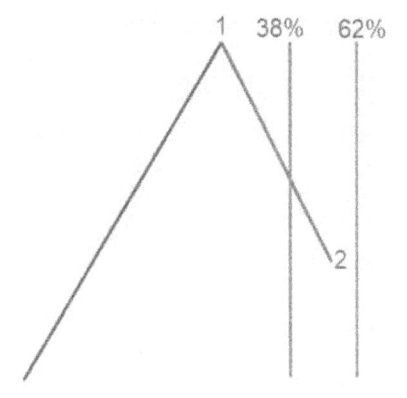

Figure 6-4: Time ratios for Wave 2

In this diagram, the upward line represents an impulse move in Wave 1 and the downward line represents the retracement in Wave 2. By using two reference points (the beginning and the end of Wave 1), we have Fibonacci time ratios plotted into the future. Most commonly, Wave 2 often takes between 38 percent and 62 percent of the time elapsed during the Wave 1 formation. Note that Wave 2 is often a simple sharp correction in the form of a zigzag, which tends to transpire fairly quickly, making it a short-lived affair. Below is a real example on a price chart.

Figure 6-5: 38% - 62% time ratio

In this example, the price action leads to a fairly deep retracement which is what we would expect for a typical Wave 2 retracement. Notice the time component in this example. The price moves into the 38 percent - 62 percent time zone, bouncing to the upside and never looking back. It eventually takes out the Wave 1 high in what certainly looks like Wave 3 price action.

## Fibonacci ratios for Wave 3

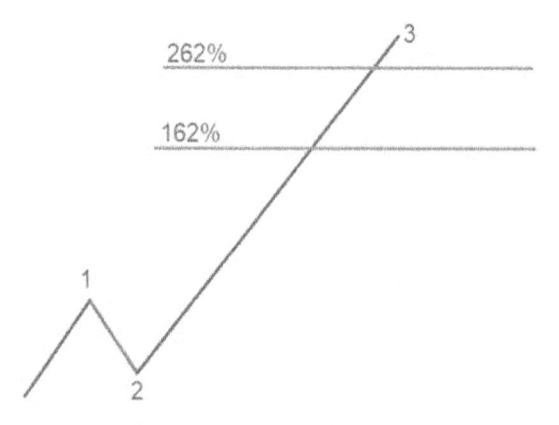

Figure 6-6: Fib ratios for Wave 3

Let's now move on to addressing the most important relationships for Wave 3. On this diagram, you can see the initial Wave 1 followed by a deep Wave 2 retracement, and a Wave 3 that is moving in the same direction as Wave 1 to the upside. Just as Wave 2 has a strong relationship with Wave 1, Wave 3 also has a strong relationship with Wave 1. In fact, of all the relationships within the impulse phase that we discuss, the relationship between Wave 1 and 3 is the most reliable and significant. To gauge the extent of the Wave 3 price move, we'll use the Fibonacci projection tool.

Remember we need three reference points to calculate the Fibonacci projection levels: swing A, swing B, and swing C. In this case, we're looking at a bullish move, so we'll start with the beginning of Wave 1 which is swing A, and move up to the end of Wave 1 which is swing B. Finally, we have the end of Wave 2 which is swing C. Once these three reference points are selected, the projection levels should appear on your charts as horizontal lines.

Now comes the important relationship. Wave 3 is often 162 percent of the length of Wave 1. Sometimes, in a very strong trending market, it will extend to 262 percent of the length of Wave 1. This will make better sense to you if you understand the characteristic of Wave 3. As an unbreakable rule, Wave 3 cannot be the shortest among impulse waves 1, 3, and 5. Next, one of the important Elliott Wave guidelines tells us that Wave 3 is often the extended wave, and as such, it tends to be the longest wave amongst Waves 1, 3, and 5. During Wave 3, many traders that were skeptical about the trend in Wave 1 have now joined the trend. As the price breaks the Wave 1 extreme, more and more traders and investors hop on the bandwagon, driving prices further in the direction of the trend. Let's take a look at one real example below.

Figure 6-7: Fib ratios for Wave 3

In this example, you can see four different Fibonacci projection levels plotted using the three reference points: the start of Wave 1, the end of Wave 1, and the end of Wave 2. First, we can see the price stalls as it reaches the 127 percent projection level. After that, the downward momentum slows one more time when it approaches the 161.8 percent level. Notice how the price comes back to test this level before making one more leg down to the 272 percent price area which acts as the strongest barrier in this case. After reaching the last key barrier, the price corrects to the upside when it enters Wave 4.

## Fibonacci ratios for Wave 4

Next on the menu, we'll discuss the most common relationships for Wave 4 in comparison with Wave 3.

Price relationship

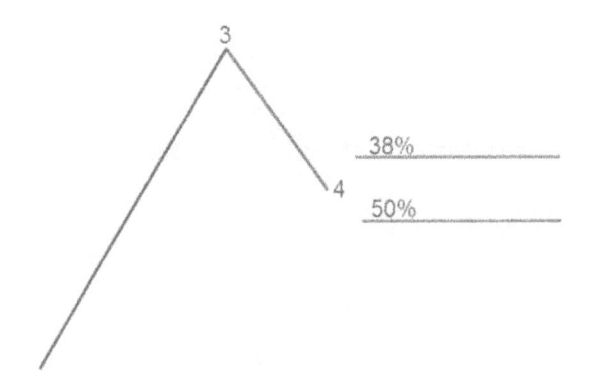

Figure 6-8: Fib ratios for Wave 4

On this diagram, you will see a bullish Wave 3 followed by the Wave 4 retracement. Wave 4 often retraces between 38 percent and 50 percent into Wave 3's territory.

Keep in mind that in a very strong trending market, Wave 4 may only retrace Wave 3 by 24 percent. However, in a large majority of cases, the 38 percent - 50 percent range is often respected and tends to be the most reliable for the purposes of executing high probability trades. As you may already know, we need to use the Fibonacci retracement tool in order to calculate these levels. The two reference points will be the start of Wave 3 and the end of Wave 3.

Comparing Wave 4 and Wave 2, you may notice that the Wave 4 retracement is shallower in most cases.

Now, let's take a look at a Wave 4 retracement on a real chart.

Figure 6-9: Fib ratios for Wave 4

On this chart, I've selected the start of Wave 3 and the end of Wave 3 as the two reference points to plot the Fibonacci retracement levels. One mistake I see some traders make when plotting the Wave 4 retracement levels is they take the start of Wave 1 instead of the start of Wave 3 as the first reference point. Make sure you don't make this mistake, otherwise the retracement outputs will be incorrectly marked on the chart. Once we've selected the correct swing points and drawn the Fibonacci retracement levels for Wave 4, we want to wait until the price reaches this level before initiating any new trades. In this particular case, prices move quite easily through the 38 percent level, but eventually found solid resistance at the 50 percent level which turned out to be the high of the Wave 4 correction.

## Time relationship

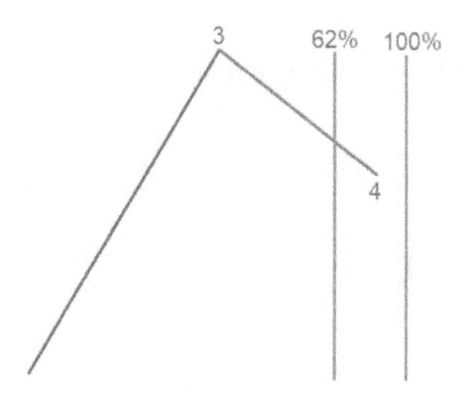

Figure 6-10: Time ratios for Wave 4

Now, let's take a look at the time relationship between Waves 3 and 4. If you recall in our earlier discussion on the time relationship between Waves 1 and 2, you'll remember that a sharp Wave 2 often takes between 38 percent and 50 percent of the time that Wave 1 takes to form. So, what about the time relationships between Waves 3 and 4? The most common time relationship between the two waves is that Wave 4 takes between 62 percent and 100 percent of the time for Wave 3 to complete. The reason for this is that Wave 4 is often a drawn-out sideways correction and may develop into a triangle or combination corrective pattern which takes quite a bit of time to unfold. This time relationship between the two waves is much more reliable than the time relationship between Wave 1 and Wave 2. It's the guideline that I believe you should really keep an eye on. Below is an example of the Fibonacci time ratios for the Wave 4 correction.

Figure 6-11: Time ratios for Wave 4

In this example, notice a deep correction in Wave 2, and a sharp upward move that follows, leading into Wave 3. All these types of thought processes and considerations should go into the evaluation of wave count. As we can see, after the extreme of Wave 3 is reached, the price begins to back off in what appears to be a sharp correction, leading into the important 62 percent - 100 percent Fibonacci time zone. The price begins to stall and consolidate in the middle of the zone and then breaks to the upside in Wave 5.

So, I hope you're beginning to appreciate the Fibonacci relationships among the different waves within the overall Elliott Wave cycle. Next, we'll continue to discover the most common Fibonacci relationships within Wave 5.

## Fibonacci ratios for Wave 5

We've covered quite a bit in this chapter, but we still have one more important wave to discuss within the impulse sequence - Wave 5. Let's go over the diagram below.

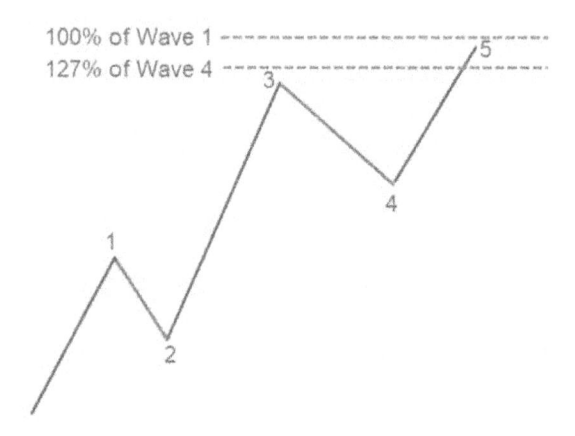

Figure 6-12: Fib ratios for Wave 5

In this illustration, you can see the five impulse waves in place. Just as Waves 2 and 3 have a strong relationship to Wave 1, so does Wave 5. But the interesting thing about Wave 5 is that it also has an important relationship with Wave 4. These two relationships should be used in tandem to create a termination zone for the end of Wave 5.

Here are the common relationships that we need to keep in mind for Wave 5. Wave 5 and Wave 1 are related by equality, meaning that the length of Wave 5 is often equal to the length of Wave 1. Additionally, Wave 5 is often a 127 percent extension of Wave 4. To make use of these relationships, we need two tools in gauging the extent of the Wave 5 price move.

The first one is the Fibonacci projection tool which we will use to project the length of Wave 1 from the end of Wave 4 to find the probable termination point of Wave 5. Referring back to the Elliott Wave guidelines, one of the waves among Waves 1, 3, and 5 will be longer than the other two, and the two shorter waves will tend towards equality. Statistically speaking, Wave 3 is often the longest wave among these three waves, meaning that Waves 1 and 5 are often of equal length. As such, the 100 percent Fibonacci projection of Wave 1 is used in finding the termination point of its related degree Wave 5.

Also, we'll need to use the Fibonacci extension tool to plot the 127 percent extension of Wave 4. We would use the end of Wave 3 and the orthodox end of Wave 4 in measuring this extension. It's important to note that the orthodox end of Wave 4 is sometimes different than the extreme of Wave 4. This is because the orthodox end refers to the termination point of the pattern which may not always be the extreme point within the pattern. Yet, from a practical matter, if you are unable to get a reliable count within the Wave 4 retracement, you could consider using the extreme of Wave 4 as the second point after plotting both of these Fibonacci studies.

Wave 5 progression often ends between the 100 percent projection level of Wave 1 and the 127 percent extension level of Wave 4.

Figure 6-13: Fib ratios for Wave 5

Turning to this price chart, you can see the length of Wave 1 which is shown with the vertical dashed line. We want to project this distance off the end of Wave 4. This is also shown on the chart by the second dashed line, expressing an equal length to the first one. Notice at the top right of the chart, we have two horizontal lines, the higher of which is the 100 percent projection of Wave 1. Based on this typical one-to-one relationship between Wave 1 and 5 within the charting software, we would select the three swing points (the beginning of

Wave 1, the end of Wave 1, and the end of Wave 4) to calculate the Wave 5 projection level.

The other border of the zone is the 127 percent extension of Wave 4. You can see how I've done that by referring to the diagonal dashed line connecting the start and the end of Wave 4. Once we've selected the proper points, the 127 percent extension level should plot on the chart. As you can see, Wave 5 ends right at the zone created by these two lines.

This marks the end of the chapter. In this chapter, we've gone over all the important Fibonacci relationships in connection with the impulse sequence. Next, we will shift our focus and start to learn the common relationships between waves in the corrective phase. Stay tuned.

# CHAPTER 7: FIBONACCI AND THE CORRECTIVE PHASE

This chapter will focus on the relationships between waves in the corrective sequence. However, before learning those relationships, let's remember a few main points about the three waves within the corrective phase of the Elliott Wave cycle.

You should now know that once Wave 5 of the impulse completes, prices will move into the corrective phase labeled A, B, and C.

The price action and psychology within the corrective phase are quite different than that during the impulse phase. Wave A kicks off the corrective phase, moving counter to the prior trend, but most traders aren't concerned about the integrity of the trend at this point. In fact, many traders view the retracement in Wave A as just another pullback within the trend, thus a good opportunity to add to their existing positions.

Once Wave A completes, prices will begin to push along in Wave B, and it will be in the direction of the larger degree trend once again. But trading in the direction of the trend in Wave B is considered a sucker's play. It may lead many traders, both inexperienced and experienced, into thinking that the market is getting ready for the next big leg within the trend, but this would not happen. Instead of a strong follow-through in Wave B, it will be a short-lived affair, and as a result, will catch many traders off guard and on the wrong side of the market. Wave B will often fail to take out the Wave 5 extreme and stop out many traders who participated in the move during this wave.

Wave C brings with it the realization by most market participants that the larger trend is likely over and a reversal is in the works. Wave C has many characteristics of Wave 3. It can often be a swift and sharp leg, and it tends to end within the span of Wave 4 of the prior impulse, or slightly beyond it. At this point, many traders are convinced that the trend has changed and positioned themselves in the direction of Wave C. It will sadly be too late for these late comers as the tide will turn and the prices will resume in the direction of the larger trend.

## Fibonacci ratios for Wave A

Let's take a look at the illustration below regarding Fibonacci ratios for Wave A retracement.

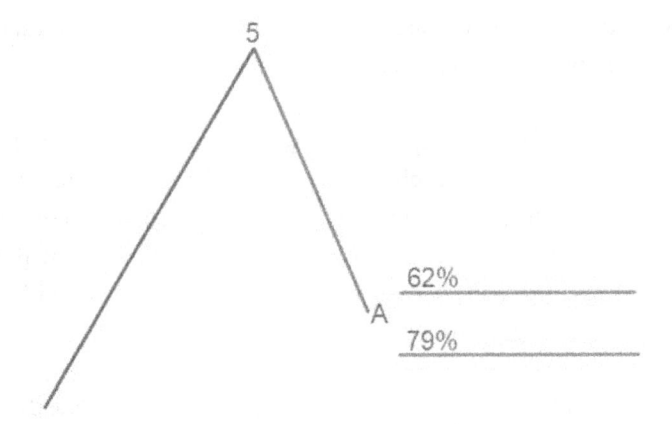

Figure 7-1: Fib ratios for Wave A

The upward line represents an impulse move in Wave 5. The completion of Wave 5 marks the end of the corresponding impulse phase. The downward line demonstrates a retracement against Wave 5, which is Wave A - the beginning of the corrective phase. We would use the Fibonacci retracement tool to calculate the most likely termination point for Wave A. Often, the retracement ends between the 62 percent and 79 percent of the length of Wave 5. Let's have a look at one example below.

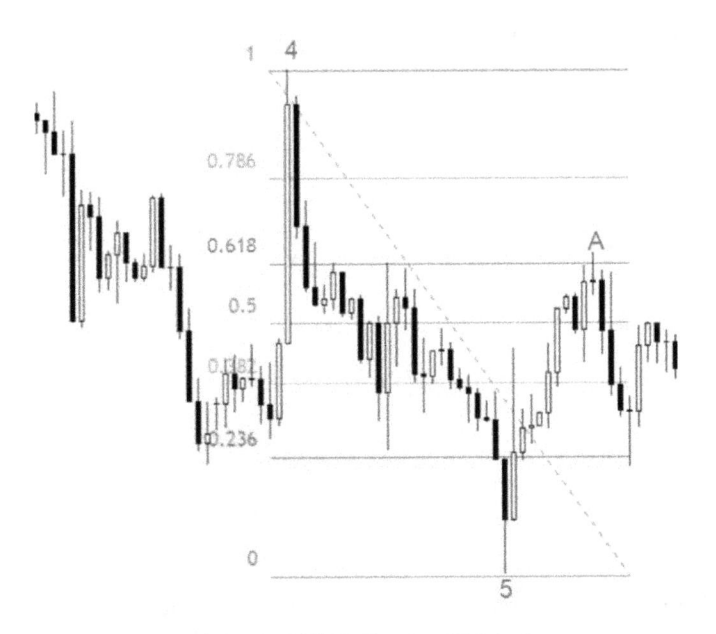

Figure 7-2: Fib ratios for Wave A

On this chart, following the end of Wave 5, the price advances as it transitions from an impulse phase to a corrective phase. Starting at the end of Wave 5, the price gradually moves past a few retracement lines before stalling at the 62 percent retracement level and reversing quite a bit into Wave B of the phase.

## Fibonacci ratios for Wave B

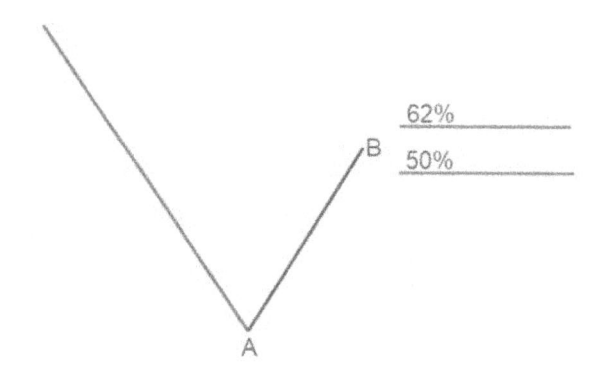

Figure 7-3: Fib ratios for Wave B

Following the completion of Wave A within the corrective phase, the price will move into Wave B. In this example, you can see an illustration of a bullish Wave B after a bearish Wave A. Since Wave B is related to Wave A in the form of a retracement, we would use the Fibonacci retracement tool to calculate the most likely termination point for Wave B using the length of Wave A. This wave often ends between 50 percent and 62 percent of the length of Wave A. Just as Wave 2 tends to move deeply into the price territory of Wave 1, Wave B tends to move deeply into the price territory of Wave A. Leaning on this type of counter-trend setup and using the Wave 5 extreme as the swing point for placing your stop-loss order is one of the highest probability trade setups that you can use in trading.

Let's take a look at an example of Wave B Fibonacci ratios on the price chart.

Figure 7-4: Fib ratios for Wave B

In this example, we have Wave 1 followed by a short-lived Wave 2. Wave 3 is characterized by a long bearish candle. After Wave 3 completes, we get a deep pullback for Wave 4, which is quite rare in the financial markets. Wave 5 is another long wave in this particular case, putting an end to the impulse sequence. Following this downward move, the corrective phase starts with a gradually upward move in Wave A before a fall in Wave B occurs right at the 50 percent retracement level.

## **Fibonacci ratios for Wave C**

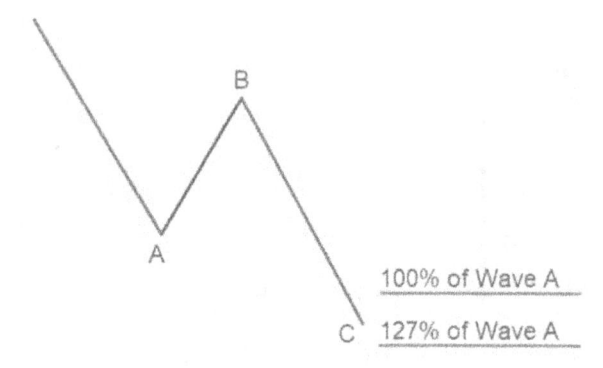

Figure 7-5: Fib ratios for Wave C

After Wave B is completed, the price will begin to trace out a path for Wave C. In this diagram, you can see an illustration of Wave C following Wave B. Wave C is related to Wave A, and since both waves move in the same direction, we would use the Fibonacci projection tool to find the probable termination point for Wave C. The most common Fibonacci relationship between Wave C and Wave A is the "equality in length". Essentially, we can expect Wave C to be of equal length as Wave A. The next most likely target would be the 127 percent projection of Wave A. Let's see what this looks like on a price chart.

Figure 7-6: Fib ratios for Wave C

On this chart, we can see the clear five-wave impulse pattern followed by Waves A-B-C of the corrective sequence. The upper line on the chart represents the 100 percent projection level while the lower line shows the 127 percent projection level. Notice how the price moved into this zone and quickly got rejected to the upside. Subsequently, a new impulse sequence was underway after this rejection.

## **What if the relations don't work?**

In real trading, there are cases when the market seems to ignore the Fibonacci levels, both in the impulse and corrective phases. Instead of being depressed about those price movements, we should take market reactions into account to better revise our market approach.

For example, if the price breaks through a level, it suggests that the reversal could occur at the next level. Obviously, it is quite a distance to extract more profits from the market. On the other hand, if the pre-determined Fibonacci points are not reached, this is a suggestion to revise our wave interpretation and count. It should be noted that waves don't have idealized structures in quite a number of cases. Traders have a few versions of current trend interpretation and stick to one until it works, or switch to another version.

We've now completed all chapters concerning the Elliott Wave principle, Fibonacci ratios, and the relationships between them. There is a lot of valuable information in the past chapters, and I've tried to present all of them in the most specific manner possible. We now have all the relevant knowledge to move into the most important part of this book which I believe is the one that you may have been waiting for.

In the following chapters, I am going to reveal all the Elliott Wave-Fibonacci-based trading strategies IN GREAT DETAIL. However, to make the last chapters the most interesting and educational ones, let's shift gears a bit and discover four powerful tools for filtering trade setups in the market. We'll refer to these tools later, but now, I recommend you download (FOR FREE) the bonus that I've prepared along with this book so that you could be in the best position to learn about proven strategies in the next chapters. Visit https://bit.ly/3xIZRqw to download for FREE.

# CHAPTER 8: TRADING STRATEGY NO.1

From this chapter, we're going to take a deep dive into the high-probability strategies that I use in my trading. They incorporate all that we've learned about Elliott Wave and Fibonacci. If there are any lessons that you may still have some difficulties wrapping your head around, I would highly suggest that you go back and revisit those lessons again because all the components that we've discussed in our journey to this point will serve as building blocks for the trading setups that I'm going to share with you.

There are five main strategies that I often trade within the Elliott Wave cycle. I've merged various analysis techniques related to Elliott Wave and Fibonacci into a trading model that offers the highest probability trading opportunities in the market. These trading techniques are the results of many years of studying, testing, applying, and refining different market movements.

## **Trade analysis**

The first setup that we will be discussing is the ***Wave 4 retracement setup***. Obviously, this particular setup will occur during Wave 4. Wave 4 is the final retracement leg within the impulse before the final push into Wave 5 occurs. The goal for trading the Wave 4 retracement is to catch the termination or near termination point of Wave 4 so that we can ride the final leg in Wave 5. Our aim is to try to exit the trade at or near the termination point of Wave 5.

If you recall from our earlier discussion on corrective patterns, Wave 4 tends to be a sideways correction, typically seen in the form of a flat, a triangle, or a combination of two. Although a zigzag can appear within a Wave 4 correction, it is not quite common.

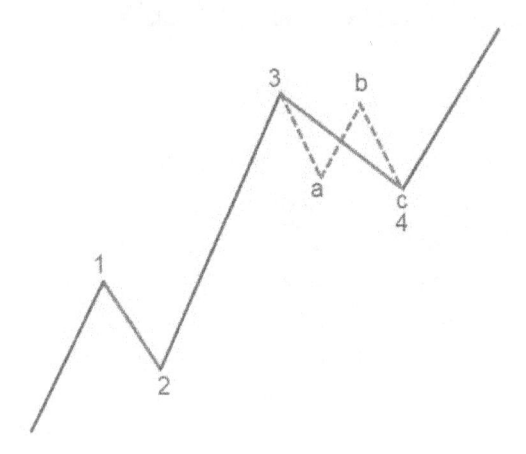

Figure 8-1: Wave 4 as a regular flat

Here's what Wave 4 looks like when it registers as a flat correction. In this particular example, we are looking at a regular flat variety. As you may recall, the regular flat trades as an A-B-C correction with a 3-3-5 subdivision. In a regular flat, Wave B retraces Wave A by at least 80 percent, and Wave C closes just below the end of Wave A.

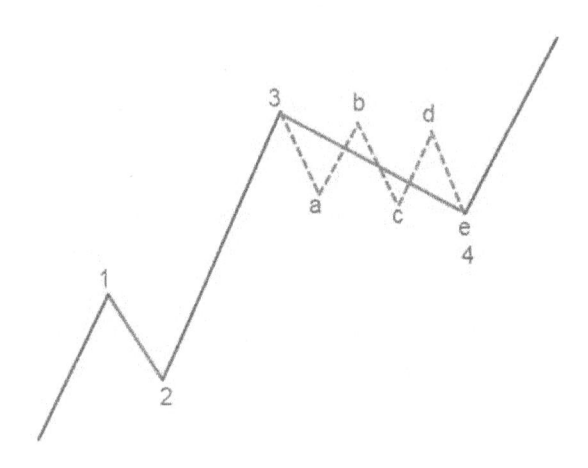

Figure 8-2: Wave 4 as a triangle

Here is an illustration of Wave 4 that unfolds as a triangle. It can occur in Wave 4 as a simple triangle as shown here or within a combination. When a triangle occurs within a double or triple combination, it can be quite a challenge to label correctly. Fortunately, a simple triangle is more prevalent and can be fairly straightforward to label. In this example, we have a contracting variety, subdividing into five waves labeled A, B, C, D, and E. We want to wait for the completion of sub-wave E within the triangle, which in turn would complete the Wave 4 correction. After that, we could take advantage of the next leg which will be the Wave 5 impulse.

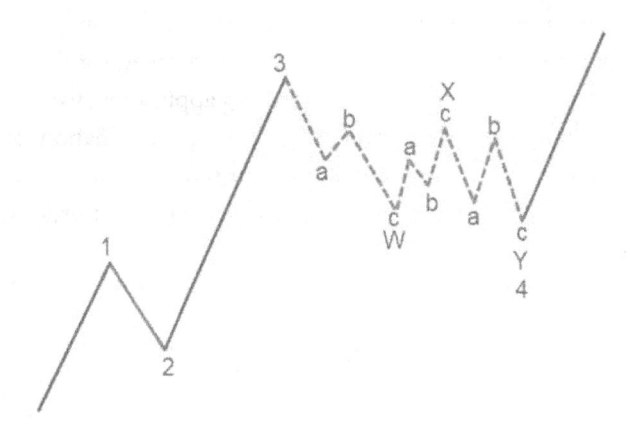

Figure 8-3: Wave 4 as a double combination

Let's now take it one notch higher and analyze a double combination within the Wave 4 correction. In this illustration, you can see an example of a double combination structure in Wave 4. Recall that double combinations are designated with the labels (W), (X), and (Y). In this particular instance, the double combination is comprised of a zigzag within the (W) leg, a zigzag within the (X) leg, and a regular flat within the (Y) leg. After a double combination is completed within Wave 4 of the uptrend, we would expect prices to move higher into Wave 5.

In the next section, we'll dive deeper into the Wave 4 retracement setup and start looking at some entry and trade management techniques.

## Trade Execution

1. Normal Wave 4

<u>Aggressive approach</u>

What can we expect in terms of the depth of the retracement during the Wave 4 correction? Statistically speaking, Wave 4 will retrace between 38 percent and 50 percent of Wave 3 in a large percentage of cases. In a strong trending market, Wave 4 may only retrace Wave 3 by 24 percent, and in some less common cases, it may retrace up to 62 percent of Wave 3. However, for the purposes of finding the end of Wave 4 from a practical trading application, we want to focus on the highest statistically significant range for the termination of Wave 4, which is between the 38 percent and 50 percent retracement of Wave 3. With that in mind, we can initiate an aggressive entry using a limit order within this reversal zone.

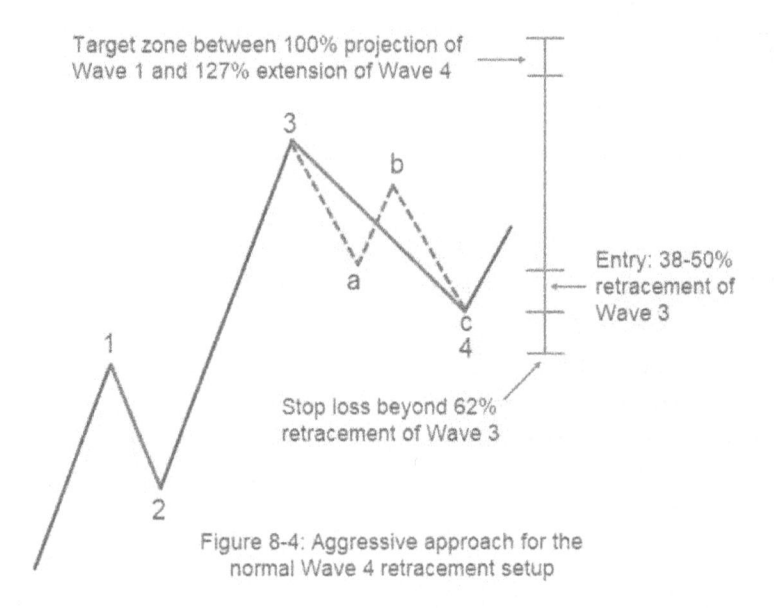

Figure 8-4: Aggressive approach for the normal Wave 4 retracement setup

This image illustrates what our strategy might look like. There are several ways to initiate an entry within this zone based on your personal preference and risk profile. Typically, I prefer to place a *limit order* that is skewed more towards the 38 percent level in this retracement zone. This area is the most important level to watch for within the Wave 4 retracement. Many times, prices would just kiss the 38 percent level and never look back. As a result, you may run the risk of missing out on the trade if you place your limit order too deep within this reversal zone.

Now that we have an area of interest in terms of initiating a new trade during the Wave 4 pullback, the next natural question is how we will manage the trade once the order gets filled?

I'm a strong believer in a set-it-and-forget-it trade management methodology, meaning that I prefer to use OCO (one-cancels-the-other) orders. Essentially, this order type allows me to simultaneously add in my stop-loss and take profit levels. Assuming the order gets filled, it will be closed automatically when either the stop-loss or target gets hit. This keeps me disciplined at all times. Keep in mind that it's easy for all of your biases to come into play and all objectivity will go out the window in trading. To protect myself against these natural inclinations that we are all going to have, I try to perform the best analysis that I can prior to actually initiating the trade.

Having said that, I may adjust my target from time to time based on the developing wave structure. However, I rarely readjust my stop-loss once I'm in a trade. If I'm wrong, I want the market to take me out of my position without having to think about it. This requires a good deal of discipline, but it's something that I've incorporated into my trading for long, which serves me very well.

Taking this into account, I prefer to place a *stop-loss* order for this setup just beyond the 62 percent retracement of Wave 3. Now, it's important to note that when I say just beyond, I'm not necessarily referring to any absolute pip amounts. Instead, it should be based on some reasonable points taking into consideration the volatility of the price chart and the time frame that you're looking at. Regarding the target zone, remember Wave 5 tends to be equal in length to Wave 1 and be a 127 percent extension of Wave 4 as measured from the Wave 4 termination point. So, the logic follows that we should look to *take profit* between the 100 percent projection level of Wave 1 and the 127.2 percent extension level of Wave 4.

Conservative approach

Now, let's see what a conservative strategy looks like.

Regarding the Wave 4 retracement setup, there may be times when you either miss an aggressive entry or may just prefer a more conservative-based entry. One distinction that I want to emphasize is that a conservative approach, whether this one or others that we will discuss later on, might not be a better trading opportunity from the risk-to-reward perspective. However, it should have a higher probability of success. Therefore, it's important that you understand the differences between the two types of approaches before selecting the method that suits you the most. Honestly, I tend to focus on the aggressive approach for the most part, but when I have either missed a potential aggressive entry or simply find that the pattern doesn't meet all pre-set criteria, I may opt to execute the setup using the conservative approach.

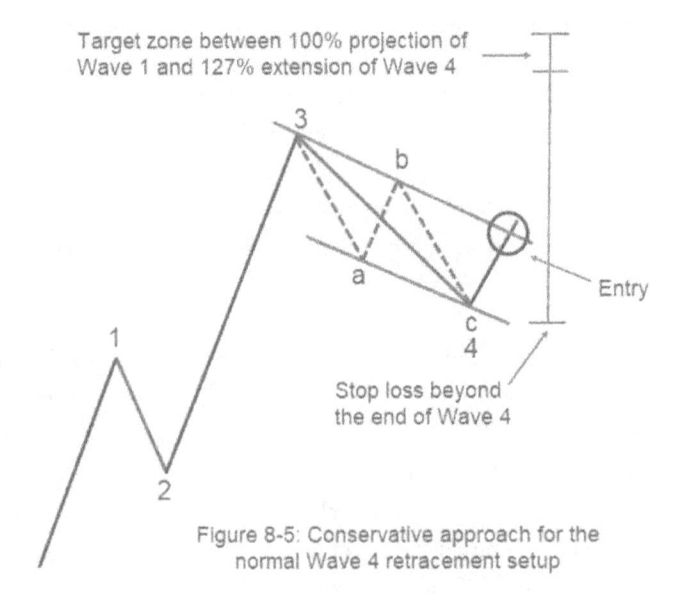

Figure 8-5: Conservative approach for the normal Wave 4 retracement setup

In this illustration, we plot a deceleration channel for the Wave 4 price action by connecting the end of Wave 3 and the end of Wave B, and then drawing a parallel line that extends from the end of Wave A. The ***entry signal*** will occur at the break of the 3-B trend line. Note that there will be other times when the price action is too messy to accurately label. During these instances, we can compose the deceleration channel using a fractal trend line drawn from the end of Wave 3 to a relevant swing fractal. We could then run the parallel of that line to construct the deceleration channel.

Notice we've drawn the 3-B trendline. This represents the upper border of the deceleration channel. The circled area represents the breakout above this level. Typically, you would want the candle that breaks the 3-B line to actually close beyond it. The stop-loss level would be placed beyond the extreme of Wave 4. The take-profit area remains the same as the aggressive approach, which consists of the 100 percent projection of Wave 1 and the 127 percent extension of Wave 4 measured from the end of Wave 4.

2. Wave 4 as a triangle

A triangle Wave 4 is considered as part of the Wave 4 retracement setup since it occurs within that corrective wave. However, we're going to be applying some different rules when the Wave 4 structure can be classified as a triangle. Let's start off by discussing the aggressive technique in this case.

Aggressive approach

Our aggressive approach is based on the relationship between Wave C and Wave E of the triangle. This relationship applies to the contracting variety. Specifically, Wave E of the triangle tends to be 62 percent of the length of Wave C of the triangle. Essentially, we can use that relationship to initiate an ***aggressive entry*** when Wave E of the triangle reaches 62 percent the length of Wave C, using the Fibonacci projection tool. To project the end of Wave E of the triangle, we would use the end of Wave B as the first reference point, the end of Wave C as a second reference point, and then apply a 62 percent Fibonacci projection of this length from the end of Wave D. This level will act as the aggressive entry point into the Wave 4 triangle setup.

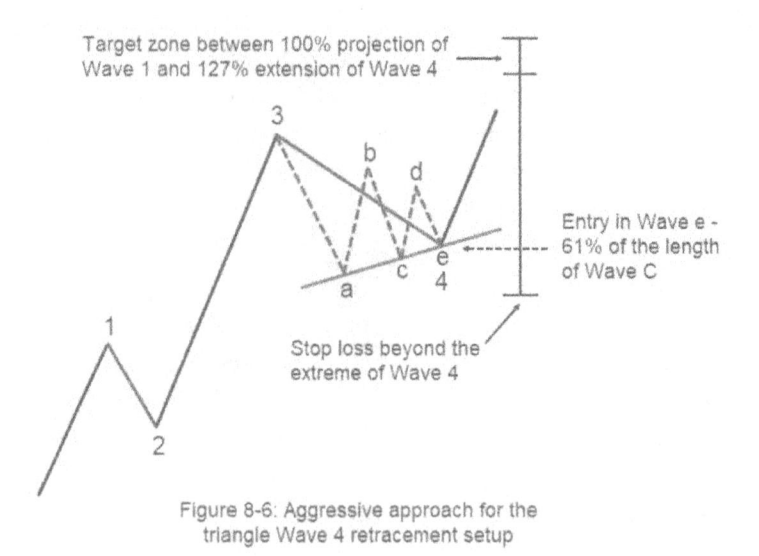

Figure 8-6: Aggressive approach for the triangle Wave 4 retracement setup

In this diagram, the circled area represents where Wave E equals 62 percent of the length of Wave C. With this aggressive approach, we would simply place a limit order at that level and wait for the order to get executed. Once this occurs, the **stop loss** would be placed beyond the extreme of Wave 4. The **target zone** remains the same: between the 100 percent projection of Wave 1 and the 127 percent extension of Wave 4. If we prepare ourselves properly to trade this setup, the risk-to-reward ratio for the trade will prove to be excellent.

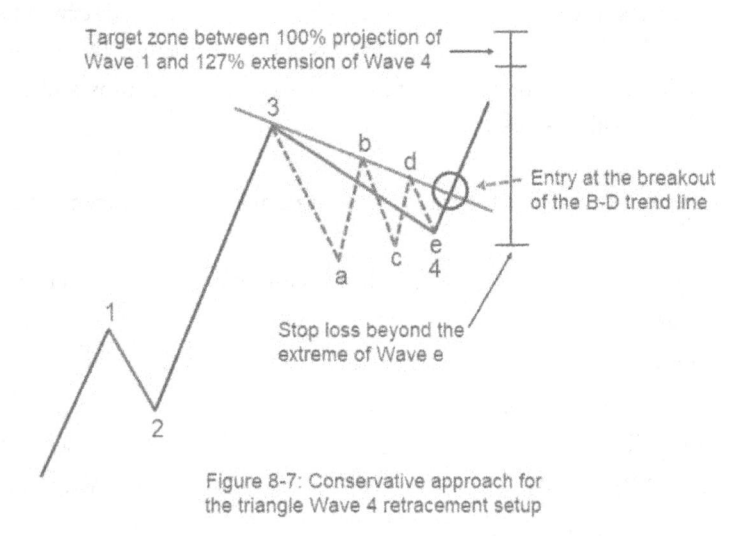

Conservative approach

Figure 8-7: Conservative approach for the triangle Wave 4 retracement setup

Let's move on to the conservative approach for the Wave 4 triangle. In case we missed the aggressive entry opportunity or just prefer to gather more evidence that we are moving into impulsive Wave 5, the conservative entry will provide us with an additional opportunity to join the progress in Wave 5. This is how the conservative approach works for the Wave 4 triangle. We will draw a trend line connecting sub-waves B and D of the triangle, and extend that forward towards the price action. The *conservative entry* is triggered when there is a candle closed beyond this B-D trend line of the triangle. This is illustrated by the circled area on the chart. Once this breakout is confirmed, you'll need to make sure that you're placing a hard stop and take profit order in the market. The *stop-loss* should be placed beyond the extreme of Wave E of the triangle, which is essentially the orthodox end of Wave 4. The *target zone* will be measured using the 100 percent projection of Wave 1 and the 127 percent extension of Wave 4, both measured from the orthodox end of Wave 4.

## Trade Toolkit

We've looked at some ways that we can recognize the Wave 4 retracement setup and some of the different techniques for executing the setup. In this section, we'll take a look at various tools to filter out sub-optimal setups and hone in on the highest quality setups.

Below is the toolkit needed for trading the normal Wave 4 retracement setup:

- The 34 SMA (34-period simple moving average): To determine the longer-term trend.
- The Base Channel: To confirm Wave 3 price action.
- The Fibonacci projection: To measure the length of Wave 3.
- A parallel channel: To provide evidence for Wave 4.
- The RSI: To confirm bull market support/ bear market resistance
- The Fibonacci retracement: To locate an aggressive entry.
- The deceleration channel: To initiate a conservative entry.
- Fibonacci extension and projection: To plot a target zone.

These are all the tools that we're going to need to make a complete evaluation of the potential viability of the normal Wave 4 retracement setup. Regarding the Wave 4 triangle formation, we'll be using many of the same tools as we would with the regular Wave 4 retracement setup with a few minor exceptions. Here's the list of tools and studies that we will rely on for trading the Wave 4 triangle formation.

- The 34 SMA (34-period simple moving average): To determine the longer-term trend.
- The Base Channel: To confirm Wave 3 price action.
- The Fibonacci projection: To measure the length of Wave 3.
- A parallel channel: To provide evidence for Wave 4.
- The RSI: To confirm bull market support/ bear market resistance
- The Fibonacci projection: To locate an aggressive entry.
- Fibonacci extension and projection: To plot a target zone.

## Trade Example 1:

We've discussed the different types of methods that we can incorporate for both the regular Wave 4 retracement setup and the Wave 4 triangle setup. Furthermore, I've shown you the most statistically significant areas for placing stop loss and take profit prices. We also talked about the toolkit that we need to carefully evaluate and analyze each potential Wave 4 setup. Now, we're going more into the practical application of these various tools and studies. You'll see how I follow a very process-oriented analytical approach that ultimately leads to qualifying the highest quality Wave 4 setups to trade. Let's begin with the first example.

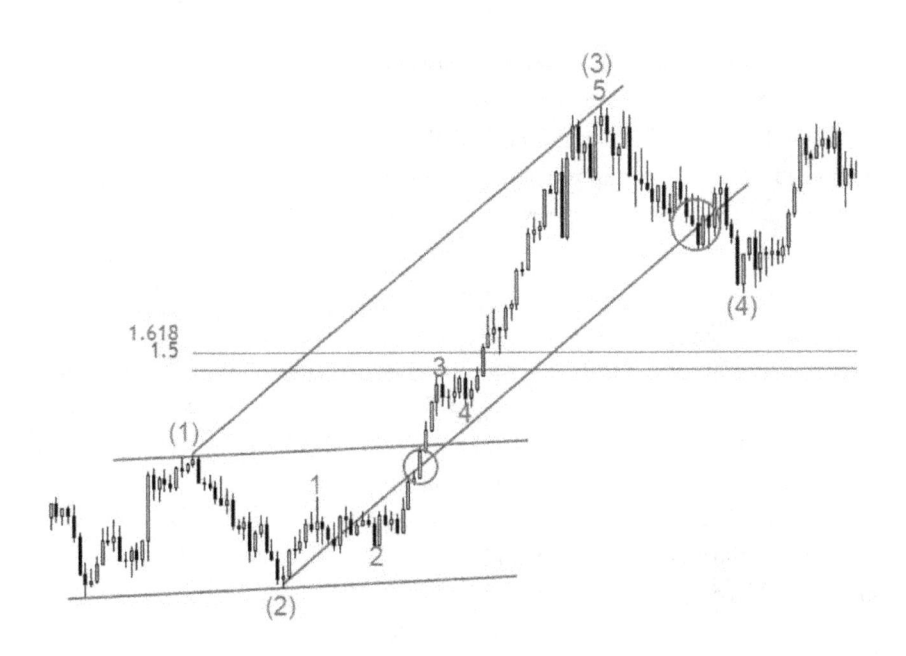

Figure 8-8: Trade analysis

On this daily Swiss Franc/Japanese Yen chart, you can see the market is in an uptrend. I've labeled the impulse sequence up to Wave (4), and also labeled the subdivisions within Wave (3). This would be my preferred wave count leading into the Wave (4) retracement. Now, let's make some assessments on the eligibility of the setup.

119

The first thing that we're going to look for is some confirmation that Wave (3) has the characteristics under the Elliott Wave theory. In other words, we want to make sure that Wave (3) is impulsive in nature by confirming a breakout of the base channel. As you may recall, the base channel is constructed by connecting a line from the start of Wave (1) to the end of Wave (2), then projecting a parallel line from the end of Wave (1). You can see the two lower channel lines on the chart above that represents this base channel. Once the base channel has been constructed, the price should close beyond it and continue to follow through in the direction of that breakout. This is characteristic of Wave 3 price action. Take note of the lower circled area that represents the breakout from the base channel and the subsequent continuation of price.

Next, I want to look for a minimum price move in Wave (3) in comparison to Wave (1). You'll remember that Wave 3 often travels 162 percent of the length of Wave 1 measured from the end of Wave 2. Taking this relationship into account, I would give it a little wiggle room, meaning that I would be satisfied with a slightly lower price projection than the 162 percent and still be comfortable labeling the price move as a Wave 3. The minimum requirement is 150 percent of the length of Wave 1. Once we've selected the start of Wave (1), the end of Wave (1), and the end of Wave (2) using the Fibonacci projection tool, we can see the 150 percent and 162 percent projection levels plotted. As you can see, Wave 3 ended far beyond the 162 percent projection level, thus satisfying our condition.

Still on the chart above, I want to know whether the price has touched the parallel trendline as it progresses in Wave (4). Just as I want to see a minimum length of Wave (3) in comparison with Wave (1), I want to see that Wave (4) has touched the parallel trend line or at least is very close to touching it. Obviously, we can see that the price has touched the lower line of the channel during its travel in Wave (4) in the chart above (the higher circled area). Hence, this condition is also satisfied.

Figure 8-9: Trade analysis

The next thing I want to refer to for a potential Wave 4 is the RSI indicator. During an uptrend, it is referred to as bull market support, and during a downtrend, it acts as bear market resistance. The RSI bull market support zone tends to occur within the 30-50 range while the RSI bear market resistance zone often occurs between the 50-70 range. Going back to the chart, as we look at a possible long aggressive entry within the 38 percent – 50 percent retracement zone of Wave (3), we want to confirm that the RSI reading is within the bull market resistance zone. Notice as prices enter into the aggressive entry zone, the recorded RSI reading is around 43.78, hence paving the way for a possible long entry.

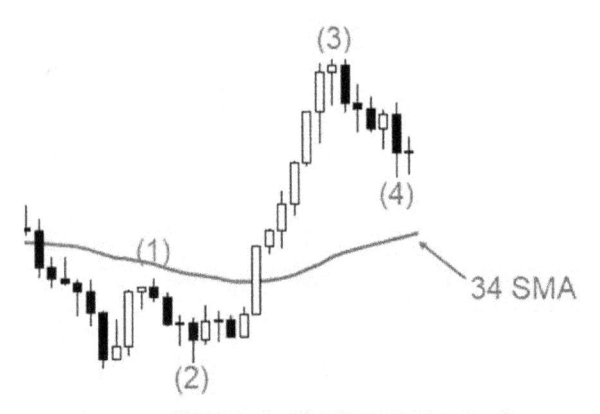

Figure 8-10: Trade analysis

Finally, I want confirmation from a higher time frame. The chart above displays the price action on the next higher time frame – the weekly chart. You can see that the Elliott Wave labels remain intact on this chart as well. This chart helps us to confirm where the price is trading in comparison with the 34-period simple moving average line, thus providing us with either a long or short bias based on the higher time frame trend. In this case, you can see that as the price was retracing into the Wave (4) correction, it remained well above the 34 SMA line, meaning that we would only watch out for a potential long position on the daily time frame.

Now that we've gone through all the different hurdles of analyzing the potential viability of trading this waveform retracement setup and have confirmed each step along the way, it's now time to execute this setup.

Aggressive approach

Figure 8-11: Aggressive approach

On this chart, notice there are three retracement lines plotted, and we'll focus on the first two lines - the 38 percent and 50 percent retracement levels of Wave (3). These two levels create the aggressive entry zone. In this case, the price touched the 38 percent level before reversing to the upside. If you decided to use the OCO order type, the stop-loss would be placed below the 62 percent retracement level of Wave (3), and the target zone is created using the 100 percent projection of Wave (1) and the 127 percent extension of Wave (4), both measured from the end of Wave (4).

There are many different options for exiting within this target zone. For example, you could exit your full position at the lower level of the zone, the higher level of the zone, or somewhere in between. Alternatively, if you prefer to scale out of your position, you could exit a portion of your position at the lower end of this range, and then the balance of your position near the upper end of the range. How and where you exit within the zone is a matter of personal preference and your desired risk parameters.

In this case, notice the distance between the two boundaries of the zone is quite big, and I normally choose to exit at the nearer end or at the exact middle of the zone in this type of market condition. As you can see, using this simple trick would have saved us from missing a handsome profit in the market.

Conservative approach

Figure 8-12: Conservative approach

Now, let's take a look and see what a conservative approach would look like in this setup. On this chart, I've plotted a deceleration channel that contains the price action within the Wave (4) correction. The conservative entry signal occurs when the price breaks out and closes beyond the deceleration channel. In this case, since we will be going long, the breakout and close should occur above the higher channel line. This is shown by the circled area on the chart. The stop-loss would be placed below the extreme of Wave (4) as illustrated by the dashed line. The target zone remains the same as with the aggressive approach.

With this, we've explored the first trade example using my trade and analysis model. I hope you're starting to get comfortable with how to trade the Wave 4 retracement setup. Let's move to the next example in connection with a Wave 4 triangle setup.

## **Trade Example 2:**

Figure 8-13: Trade analysis

Turning our attention to this chart which shows the price action for the New Zealand Dollar/Swiss Franc pair on the daily time frame, you can see we've labeled Waves (1), (2), (3), and (4). Additionally, you can see the subdivision within Wave (3) labeled. Furthermore, if we look at the price action within Wave (4), we can recognize a triangle formation with a long sideways price action. Once we recognize the triangle pattern within the fourth wave, we would start to go through our checklist process and start using the toolkit to confirm whether this setup is a good trade opportunity.

First, let's pay attention to the base channel. Notice where the breakout below this base channel occurs, which is shown by the circled area on the chart. We get a nice breakout to the downside followed by a continuation in the bearish direction. Also, notice the net traveled in Wave (3) compared to Wave (1). Projecting the length of Wave (1) off the end of Wave (2) gives us the minimum requirement for Wave (3) as shown by the upper horizontal line on the chart. The price easily reaches this minimum requirement for Wave (3). Hence, with these two filters validated, we can be confident that the labeling for Wave (3) is most likely correct.

Still, we have an acceleration channel to confirm Wave (4) price action. Notice how the upper line within the channel is violated as Wave (4) is in progress. This satisfies the minimum requirement for Wave (4). At the time this upper line of the parallel channel was touched, we could not be for sure that a triangle formation was in the works. As Wave (4) progresses further, it became increasingly evident that the Wave (4) correction was indeed a triangle formation.

Figure 8-14: Trade analysis

Next, let's see what we can gather from the RSI indicator. On this chart, you can see the RSI indicator line was mostly trading below the 50 percent level during the formation of the triangle. However, at the end of Wave E, the RSI reading is slightly above the mid-point level, thus confirming a strong level of resistance for this underlying downtrend.

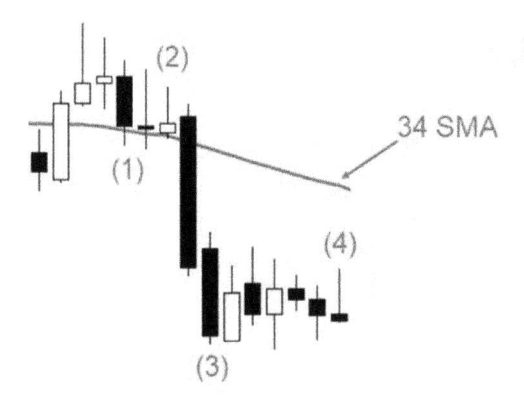

Figure 8-15: Trade analysis

Finally, we want to seek confirmation from the 34 SMA indicator for a bigger picture of the market. To do this, we switch to the next higher time frame - the weekly chart. Since the triangle formation within the impulse is occurring in an overall downtrend, it is signaling further price weakness as can be seen on the daily chart. We've known that when trading a possible Wave 4 setup, we want to trade in the direction of the longer-term trend. Notice that the current price is trading below the 34 SMA line, confirming the triangle structure on the daily chart aligns with the longer-term trend on the higher time frame. We're now ready to trade the Wave 4 retracement setup.

## Aggressive approach

Figure 8-16: Aggressive approach

Let's take a look at the aggressive approach. You've known that for a triangle Wave 4, the aggressive approach calls for entering a limit order when the price within Wave E reaches a length equivalent to 62 percent of Wave C. Since we're looking for a short trade, we enter a sell limit order at the horizontal line within Wave E of the triangle. Notice how the price kisses that level several times before getting rejected back down. In this case, the 62 percent level is an extremely important level to watch as the triangle pattern completes.

After the sell limit order is triggered on this trade setup, we would need to shift our focus to the trade exits by determining the stop-loss and the take-profit prices.

***Stop-loss:*** In this case, we would want to place a stop-loss beyond the extreme of Wave (4) (or Wave A of the triangle). This level is represented by the dashed horizontal line.

***Targets:*** One of the two components in determining the target zone is the 100 percent relationship between Waves (1) and (5), and that level would serve as the lower border of the zone. The second component that creates the target zone would be the 127 percent Fibonacci extension of Wave (4). As you can see, after Wave E within the triangle completes, the price begins to trade lower. It easily entered the target zone, and then slightly breached the lower end of the zone with several indecision candles. Regardless of where you placed your profit-taking level within this zone, it would have resulted in a profitable trade.

Conservative approach

Figure 8-17: Conservative approach

Let's now see how this setup would unfold had we used the conservative approach. You can see the B-D trend line plotted. We want to wait for the price to break and close below the B-D trend line. That breakout is represented by the circled area on the chart. As soon as the breakout candle closes below the B-D trend line, we would enter a sell market order. The stop loss is best placed beyond Wave E of the triangle as shown by the dashed horizontal line. The price easily declines into the target zone which is the same as with the aggressive approach.

By now, you should be quite familiar with how to trade the Wave 4 retracement setups. It's a core setup within my trading arsenal, and the one that offers a very favorable risk-to-reward profile. In the following chapter, we'll move on to learning the next trading setup during the transition to the corrective phase.

# CHAPTER 9: TRADING STRATEGY NO.2

## Trade analysis

We're moving into the second type of trading setup within the Elliott Wave cycle which occurs within the Wave 5 position. Wave 5 will be the final push in the direction of the overall trend. It typically takes out the extreme of Wave 3 and terminates within a zone that's created by the 100 percent relationship of Waves 1 & 5 and the 127 percent Fibonacci extension of Wave 4. We learned a lot about this target zone during the Wave 4 trade setup.

The setup I focus on within Wave 5 is the ending diagonal. Recall that an ending diagonal can occur in the Wave 5 position of an impulse, or the Wave C position of an A-B-C correction. When Wave 5 carves out an ending diagonal, we want to act to take advantage of a counter-trend price reaction. As a side note, although ending diagonals also occur in the Wave C position, I typically don't like to trade those setups as they aren't nearly as reliable or profitable as those that occur in the Wave 5 position. Finally, as for our setup naming convention, I simply refer to an ending diagonal that presents itself in the Wave 5 position as a ***Wave 5 diagonal*** setup.

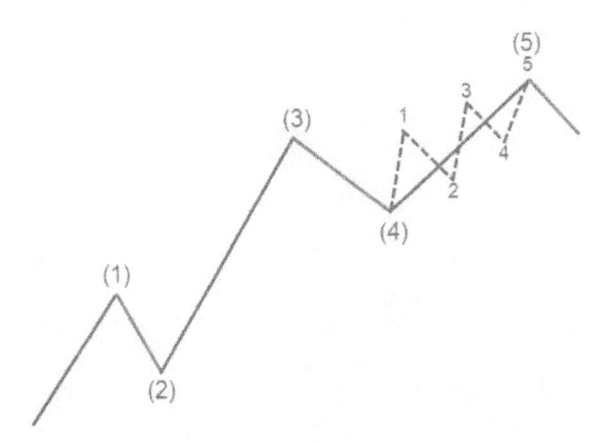

Figure 9-1: Wave 5 as an ending diagonal

Taking a closer look at this illustration, you can see Wave (5) unfold as an ending diagonal. We've discussed ending diagonals and the substructure in quite some detail in earlier chapters. Hence, this is just a very quick refresher. You should remember that the ending diagonal consists of five legs labeled (1) through (5). Moreover, it is a motive wave, meaning that it moves in the direction of the overall trend. Additionally, the ending diagonal subdivides into three waves within each of its five legs.

In the chart above, I've labeled this impulse using the intermediate degree and labeled the subdivision within Wave (5) as well. Just as with an impulse, Waves 1, 3, and 5 of the ending diagonal will move with the trend while Waves 2 and 4 of the diagonal move oppositely. You'll need to draw a line that connects the Waves 1-3 and another line that connects the Waves 2-4 within the diagonal structure. Another important characteristic that is often seen in a Wave 5 diagonal is a price throwover which occurs as prices make one final push beyond the 1-3 trend line.

## Trade Execution

As we dive into the Wave 5 trading setup, we need to make a concrete plan for entering the trade, placing a logical stop loss, and locating the optimal target zone.

## Aggressive approach

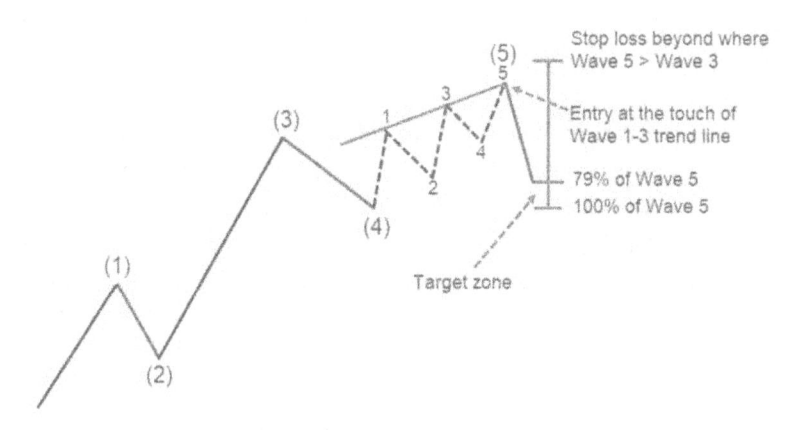

Figure 9-2: Aggressive approach

Firstly, once we can confidently label Waves (1) through (4) of the impulse sequence, and an emerging diagonal being traced out within Wave (5) of the impulse, then I begin to watch for Waves 1 through 4 of the diagonal form before looking for an entry at the touch of the 1-3 trend line or just before it. In this illustration, you can see the diagonal line which connects Waves 1-3 of the diagonal structure. The ***aggressive entry*** into this setup would occur as the final Wave 5 of the diagonal moves towards and touches the 1-3 trend line. This will often complete Wave 5 of the diagonal, and also complete Wave (5) in the impulse sequence. Our aim is to catch the turning point near the extreme high during an uptrend, and similarly to catch the turning point near the extreme low during a downtrend.

Normally, you need to be very careful when trying to pick tops in a bull market and bottoms in a bear market. Most times, I would say it's best to steer clear of such actions. However, when an ending diagonal within the Wave (5) position appears, we can stack the odds in our favor with this type of high-risk counter-trend trade. This is one of the few times that it makes a lot of sense to fade the overall trend.

Moving on to the ***stop-loss order.*** Placing a stop loss should make logical sense from the perspective of the Elliott Wave Principle and the relationship between waves within the overall structure. With that in mind, you may guess where the stop-loss should be placed in the context of this aggressive approach. We've known that within the diagonal structure, Wave 3 will be shorter than Wave 1, and Wave 5 will be shorter than Wave 3. Hence, it would make a lot of sense to place a stop loss beyond the price where Wave 5 will be bigger than Wave 3.

What about the *target zone*? If you recall from earlier sections on wave relationships, you'll remember that Wave A is often a 62 percent - 79 percent retracement of Wave 5. Obviously, that's the wave that we're looking to capture as it's the one that immediately follows the end of Wave (5) of the impulse sequence. However, in this illustration, the target zone is composed of the 79 percent and 100 percent retracement levels of Wave (5). Why does the discrepancy appear here?

Well, when Wave (5) completes, Wave (A) will look to retrace about 62 percent to 79 percent of Wave 5. But when Wave (A) is preceded by a diagonal structure in the Wave (5) position, it can be a much sharper reaction – the one that often pushes price back to the beginning of the diagonal formation. Under those circumstances, we would expect a deeper retracement during the Wave (A) correction. As such, we choose the 79 percent – 100 percent retracement zone of Wave (5) as the most likely target following a Wave (5) ending diagonal.

Conservative approach

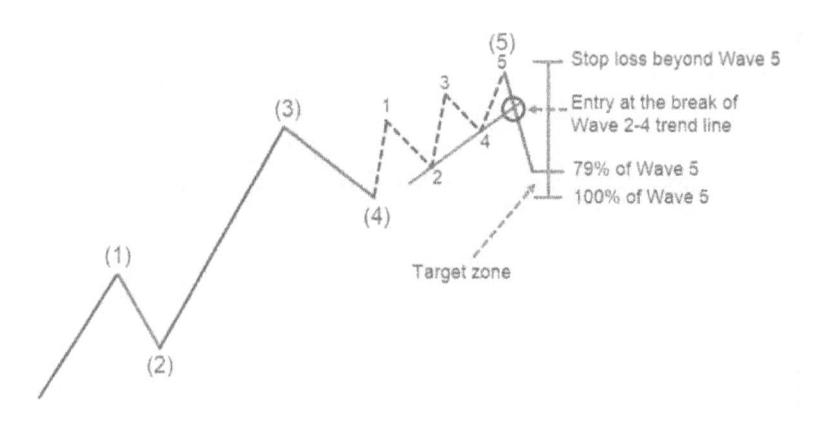

Figure 9-3: Conservative approach

Let's now turn our attention to the conservative approach for the ending diagonal. Unlike the 1-3 trend line that's of critical importance for the aggressive approach, the 2-4 trend line within the diagonal will be the key trend line for the conservative approach. First, we need to draw the 2-4 trend line within the diagonal structure as Wave 5 within the diagonal is progressing. More specifically, once the price reaches the 1-3 trend line and then begins to reverse, we'll want to make sure the 2-4 trend line is already in place. Next, we wait for the price to break and close beyond the line to trigger a *trade entry*. In any case, once the price breaks the 2-4 trend line of the ending diagonal, we should confirm that with a candle closing beyond that level before executing on the entry. The circled area on this illustration shows where the conservative entry would occur within the fifth wave ending diagonal.

The *stop loss* would be placed beyond the Wave 5 extreme. This would be labeled as Wave 5 of (5), completing the fifth wave of the diagonal structure within the fifth wave of the larger degree impulse structure. Typically, I want to use the average true range indicator, also referred to as the ATR indicator, to help me assess the volatility of the market. Normally, I like to use one ATR calculation based on the 14-period lookback and add that pip value to the end of the designated Wave 5 for the stop-loss price. This can often help prevent a premature stop-out in case the diagonal structure extends further. In case the diagonal does extend further, we may need to assess the count for the sub-waves, and adjust the 2-4 trend line accordingly.

Regarding the *profit-taking*, it would be the same as in the aggressive approach.

Note: There may be instances when the breakout appears with an extremely strong candle, such as a marubozu candle, and extends far into the price territory in the direction of the trade. When this happens, you may need to evaluate the risk-to-reward ratio to ensure that the trade setup still provides a viable opportunity. In case it doesn't, or you prefer to wait for a better entry, you may want to wait for a possible pullback after the breakout for a more favorable execution price. Having said that, in a good percentage of cases, you may run the risk of the price failing to pull back due to the swift nature of the price move. In any case, you will need to decide which scenario works better for you as the event unfolds. This can only be done once you've taken a large number of trades.

## **Trade Toolkit**

Here are some of the things that we need to keep in mind when trading the Wave 5 diagonal setup. Unlike the Wave 4 retracement setup which is a trend continuation play, the Wave 5 diagonal setup is a counter-trend play. Essentially, you could think of the Wave 5 diagonal setup as one where we are looking to fade complacency after a prolonged uptrend and buy from panic-stricken traders and investors after a prolonged downtrend. The momentum behind the Wave 5 progression will be much more subdued than the momentum during the Wave 3 progression. This will often register as a divergence on the awesome oscillator and many other momentum indicators during an uptrend. We'll often see a bearish divergence pattern as price makes a higher high in Wave 5 as compared to Wave 3 while the awesome oscillator makes a lower high during the same time. Conversely, we'll often see a bullish divergence pattern as price makes a lower low in Wave 5 as compared to Wave 3 while the awesome oscillator makes a higher low during the same time.

Wave 5 will always be a motive wave, meaning that it can either be of impulse form or a diagonal structure. Now, when the substructure appears as a diagonal formation within Wave 5, it provides a higher probability trade setup than other Wave 5 formations. Sometimes, I've seen the target zone reached within just a few bars after the 2-4 trend line break. Although this is not always the case nor the typical occurrence, it does happen from time to time. This demonstrates the powerful nature of the pattern.

Let's now take a look at the toolkit that we require for the Wave 5 diagonal setup. When we are fairly confident that a diagonal formation is emerging within the Wave 5 position, we'll begin labeling the sub-waves that compose the diagonal structure. Aside from taking all the information that we know about diagonal structures in labeling, we will want to hone in on some other complementary tools in filtering down to those setups that will provide the best trading opportunities. These include:

- Base channel: To confirm the Wave 3 price action.
- Fibonacci Projection: To measure the length of Wave 3.
- Awesome Oscillator: To confirm divergence between Wave 5 and Wave 3.
- Trend line: To locate both aggressive and conservative entry triggers.
- Fibonacci Retracement: To plot the target zone.

Now, let's move on to looking at some real chart examples using the discussed technique.

## Trade Example 1

Figure 9-4: Trade analysis

On this Euro/Japanese Yen chart, we can see a downtrend has been in progress for quite some time. I've labeled the impulse sequence using the intermediate degree. Also, notice the five legs that comprise the ending diagonal labeled 1 through 5. Once we were able to recognize that a diagonal pattern was emerging in the Wave (5) position and labeled the first four waves within the diagonal, we could begin to analyze some other related complementary tools and studies to help us in determining the suitability of trading this potential setup.

We'll start off by taking a closer look at the base channel on the intermediate degree trend. Notice the base channel at the top left of the chart due to a fairly short Wave 1 in this example. The price easily breaks and closes below the base channel as indicated by the circled area, confirming the Wave (3) price action.

Next, we'll turn to the Fibonacci projection tool to measure the length of Wave (3) as compared to Wave (1). As you may recall, the minimum requirement that I want to see for Wave (3) price action is a 150 percent projection of Wave (1) measured from the end of Wave (2). The price was able to reach this minimum level shortly after the base channel breakout to the downside. Hence, with these two analytical methods for confirming Wave (3) price action completed, we can now be confident that the labeled Wave (3) is most likely correct.

What I'd like to confirm next is whether Wave (5) has moved beyond Wave (3). In fact, it's not a requirement for a tradable Wave (5) under the Elliott Wave theory (note that even if Wave (5) fails to complete beyond Wave (3), we still have a truncated Wave (5)), but it is highly recommended that Wave (5) takes out the extreme of Wave (3) with this particular strategy. Again, we're only concerned with executing on the highest probability setups. In this example, Wave (5) does move below the extreme of Wave (3), and the requirement for this filter has been met.

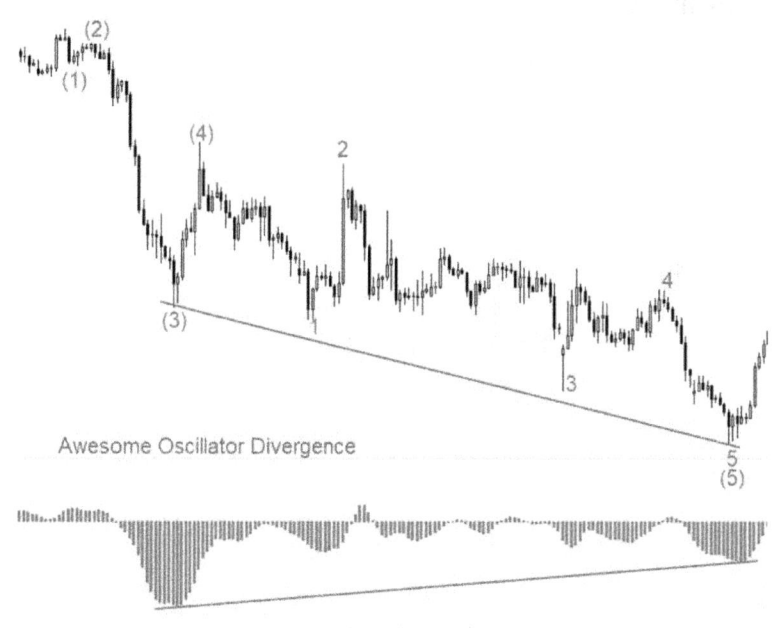

Figure 9-5: Trade analysis

Let's now take a look at the awesome oscillator as the final filter. As I mentioned earlier, the divergence pattern is an important indication of a likely turning point in the price action. Once we can confirm a divergence between Waves (3) and (5) and the awesome oscillator, it will further bolster the evidence for initiating this counter-trend setup. Notice how prices are moving lower towards the end of the intermediate wave while the awesome oscillator is registering higher lows during the same period. This tells us that the current trend is weakening. As such, a turning point may be imminent. Hence, we can conclude that this particular opportunity presents a solid trade setup.

## Aggressive approach

Figure 9-6: Aggressive approach

Firstly, we would draw a trend line that connects the end of Waves 1 and 3 of the ending diagonal to create the 1-3 trend line, and also plot a trend line that connects the end of Waves 2 and 4 of the diagonal to create the 2-4 trend line. Taking a closer look at the 1-3 trend line, the aggressive entry signal would be triggered as the price touches this trend line. In this example, you can see where that occurs as shown by the circled area. The price touches the 1-3 trend line, and then immediately reverses. The stop loss would be placed at the level where the length of Wave 5 of the diagonal would be greater than the length of Wave 3. The target zone is created using the 79 percent and 100 percent retracement levels of Wave (5).

## Conservative approach

Figure 9-7: Conservative approach

Now, let's see how we could have traded this setup using the conservative approach. The conservative entry for the Wave 5 diagonal setup calls for a breakout and close above the 2-4 trend line. With this condition met, it would trigger the conservative long entry into this trade. We would want to place a market buy order at the opening of the following candle.

With this approach, the stop loss would be placed below the Wave 5 extreme. Notice that the stop loss level allows for some room below the labeled Wave 5 which compensates for the volatility within the market. We don't want to simply put the stop loss a few pips below the termination point of the diagonal just in case the structure extends a bit further. We use the same target zone for the conservative approach as we did with our aggressive approach. You can see how the price slightly violated the upper end of the zone before reversing.

## Trade Example 2

Figure 9-8: Trade analysis

I hope you've become familiar with analyzing and trading the Wave 5 diagonal setup. On this Australian Dollar/Canadian Dollar chart, you can see an uptrend that consists of a five-wave impulse pattern of the intermediate degree. Notice Wave (2) retraces deeply into the territory of Wave (1). Then, we get a strong rally in Wave (3) that appears to be much stronger in momentum than the preceding price action in Wave (1). Wave (4) appears to be elongated as expected. In this case, the formation of Waves (2) and (4) follows the guideline of alternation.

Following the end of Wave (4), the price begins to move higher in a fairly sluggish manner. As the price advance occurs, it becomes increasingly apparent that the price action is carving out an ending diagonal in the Wave (5) position.

Let's now take this analysis a bit further and start looking at some related tools that can assist us in qualifying the setup. As before, we'll start with the base channel. Notice that the price breaks out and closes above the base channel as shown by the circled area. Subsequently, there is a strong follow-through that contributes to further price advance. This is a strong indication that what we are looking at resembles a typical Wave (3) price action.

Next, we'll use the Fibonacci projection. Plotting the Fibonacci projection tool using the start of Wave (1), the end of Wave (1), and the end of Wave (2) will allow us to locate the minimum requirement for Wave (3) – the 150 percent projection of Wave (1) projected from the end of Wave (2). The lower line in the figure shows where this minimum requirement for Wave (3) would have been met. With these, we've had confirmation from both the base channel breakout and the Fibonacci projection tool that the Wave (3) is in fact displaying characteristic price actions.

The next part of the process is to check whether Wave (5) has exceeded the extreme of Wave (3). Again, we don't want to trade a truncated Wave (5). Referring closely to the higher part of the chart above, it's clear that Wave (5) has moved beyond the extreme high of Wave (3). This actually occurred during the first leg of the diagonal structure, however, at that time, we couldn't have known that the emerging price action was likely leading to an ending diagonal structure. As the price action progressed forward, it became increasingly evident that an ending diagonal pattern was being carved out within the Wave (5) position. Let's now see if we can gather any additional information from the awesome oscillator during the progression of Wave (5).

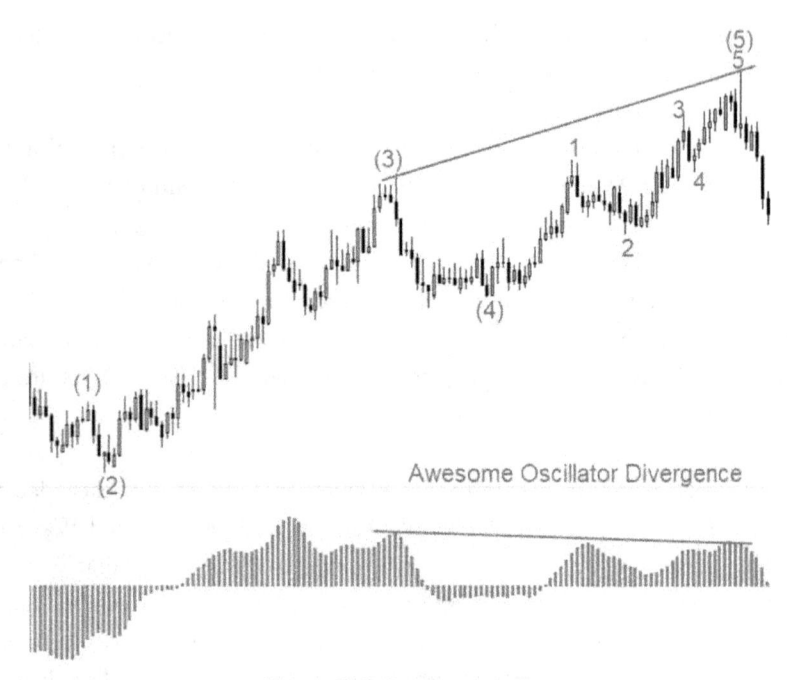

Figure 9-9: Trade analysis

From this chart, you can see that the high of Wave (3) corresponds to a high reading on the awesome oscillator. As prices move higher in Wave (5), notice how the awesome oscillator registers lower highs. This creates a bearish divergence pattern between Wave (5) price action and the awesome oscillator. At this point, all of the studies within our toolkit for the Wave (5) ending diagonal are pointing to a probable end of the prevailing uptrend and cluing us into the presence of a high probability setup. The next phase would be to find the best location for entering into this particular setup.

## Aggressive approach

Figure 9-10: Aggressive approach

The aggressive approach calls for executing an entry order at the touch of the 1-3 trend line of the diagonal structure. If you refer to the higher trend line on this chart, you can see where that touch occurs. In this instance, a sell order would be initiated upon the touch of the trend line. The stop loss would have been placed where the length of Wave 5 exceeds the length of Wave 3. This level is represented by the horizontal line at the top of the chart. The target zone is represented by the 79 percent and 100 percent retracement levels of Wave (5). Right after the aggressive entry, the price broke the 2-4 trend line to the downside and quickly moved into this target zone.

Conservative approach

Figure 9-11: Conservative approach

With a conservative approach, we would have to wait for a breakout and close below the 2-4 trend line as can be seen within the circled area. Also, the stop loss is placed above the Wave 5 extreme of the diagonal structure which also corresponds to the end of the five-wave impulse of the intermediate degree. As such, that area is labeled as 5 of (5). The target zone remains the same for both the aggressive and conservative approaches. As can be seen, the price entered the target zone easily.

This concludes our study on an excellent counter-trend strategy that you can take advantage of when the right opportunity comes along. In the next chapter, we'll continue to move along the corrective phase to discover another great trading opportunity.

# CHAPTER 10: TRADING STRATEGY NO.3

### Trade analysis

Up until now, we've discussed the Wave 4 retracement setup and the Wave 5 diagonal setup. Now, we'll move on to the third setup which occurs at the end of Wave B. I refer to it as the **Wave B retracement setup**.

As we've learned, Wave 5 is the last push in the impulse sequence. Also, if a diagonal structure occurs within the Wave 5 position, we know that a solid trade opportunity may exist. We need to confirm the overall structure of the diagonal along with the other technical studies that I shared with you for analyzing the viability of a Wave 5 diagonal setup.

Once Wave 5 completes, the corrective phase will begin, starting with Wave A. This will be followed by Wave B which will move in the direction of the prior trend. However, it will fail to follow through, and as such, it will provide an excellent opportunity for a contrarian trade.

As Elliott Wave traders, we learn to recognize this recurring pattern and see it over and over again. We will be confidently selling to the uninformed bulls during the uptrend and buying from the uninformed bears during the downtrend. This opportunity will allow us to take advantage of the Wave C leg which often has many of the same characteristics as Wave 3 of the impulse. As such, the Wave B retracement setup offers a solid trading opportunity with a very discernible pattern along the wave cycle. With that, let's move into taking a closer look at some different ways that we can expect Wave B to transpire.

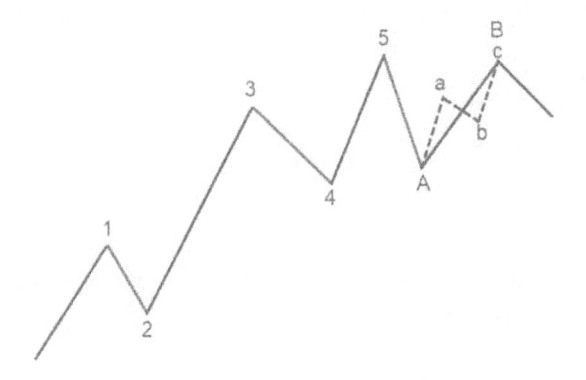

Figure 10-1: Wave B as a zigzag

One of the common ways for Wave B to unfold is as a simple zigzag as illustrated in the image above. Notice the lowercase a-b-c notation for the zigzag which occurs within the larger Wave B. Remember that the zigzag also has a 5-3-5 subdivision. Sometimes, you may need to zoom down to a smaller time frame to actually see the smaller subdivisions.

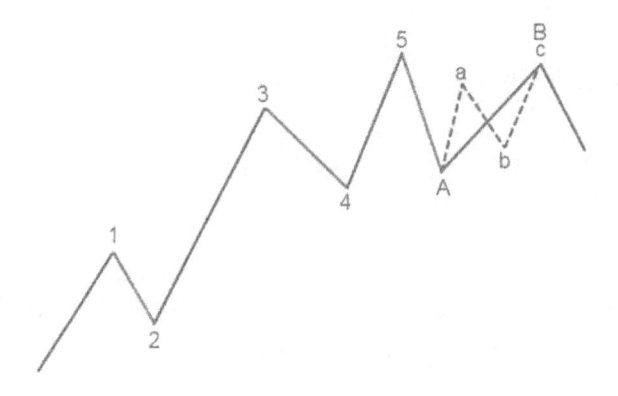

Figure 10-2: Wave B as a regular flat

Here's the illustration of Wave B as a regular flat. Notice the subdivision of the regular flat labeled a-b-c within the larger Wave B correction. In a regular flat, Wave b will retrace Wave a by at least 80 percent, and then Wave c will move slightly beyond the end of Wave a.

148

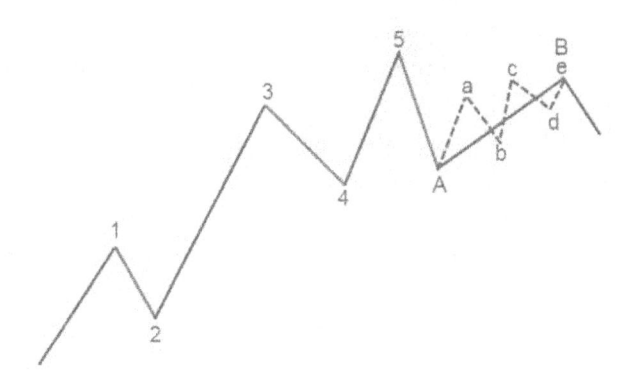

Figure 10-3: Wave B as a triangle

Wave B can also be in the form of a triangle pattern. In this illustration, after Wave 5 completes, there is a sharp move down in Wave A. This is followed by a low volatility period where the price action appears to be range-bound. When this occurs within the Wave B position, it's often a sign that a triangle may be in the works. The triangle consists of five legs labeled a, b, c, d, and e. Just as with a triangle in the Wave 4 position, the triangle in the Wave B position would be followed by one more leg that will move in the direction from which it came.

## Trade Execution

What are the most common Fibonacci ratios that we can expect for the Wave B retracement? Well, Wave B typically retraces between 50 percent and 62 percent of Wave A. I find that in a larger percentage of cases, Wave B will typically retrace closer to the 62 percent level than the 50 percent level. When prices do turn within this retracement zone, we can often expect the entire A-B-C corrective to be a zigzag formation. There will be times when Wave B will be a deeper retracement, such as a 79 percent retracement level. Normally, when this type of deep retracement occurs, the market will carve out some variation of the flat pattern for the larger A-B-C correction.

One technique that can also help us in knowing whether the corrective A-B-C structure will form a zigzag or flat is by studying the subdivisions within Wave

A. More specifically, if Wave A of the corrective phase appears to subdivide into three smaller waves, it's more likely that the entire structure will be a flat, and as such, Wave B could retrace beyond our designated retracement zone. On the other hand, if Wave A of the corrective appears to subdivide into five smaller waves, it's more likely that the entire corrective structure will be a zigzag, and Wave B will probably terminate within our designated retracement zone. Having said that, it's not always possible to recognize a clear subdivision within the A leg of the corrective phase. However, it's certainly something that you should watch out for since it could help you in anticipating the depth of the B leg.

## Aggressive approach

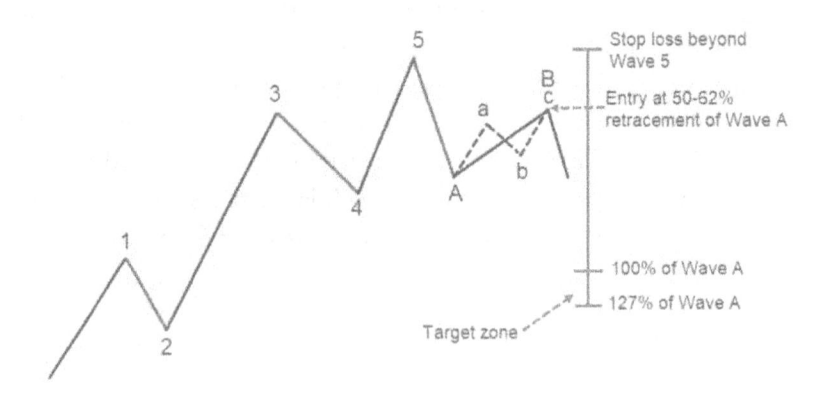

Figure 10-4: Aggressive approach

Here's what the aggressive method would look like for the Wave B retracement setup. Though this illustration is not exactly the scale, it can provide us with the necessary framework for understanding the basic mechanics of the technique. In this particular example, we have a zigzag formation within the larger Wave B retracement. The aggressive approach would call for a *limit order entry* when the price enters the 50 percent - 62 percent retracement zone during its progress in Wave B.

A *stop-loss* order would be placed beyond the extreme of Wave 5 as shown in the illustration. This level provides a logical area to protect the trade in case our overall bias is correct but the Wave B correction leads to a deeper retracement.

As mentioned earlier, this would be typical if the entire A-B-C corrective is poised to form a regular flat. In such a case, the stop placement beyond the Wave 5 extreme would provide us with this extra breathing room on the trade.

The **target zone** for the strategy takes into account the important relationship between Wave A and Wave C. Specifically, Wave C will often travel a distance equivalent to that of Wave A. This is the most common relationship between Wave C and Wave A. The next most common relationship seen among the two waves is that Wave C will extend around 127 percent of the length of Wave A. As such, I incorporate these two projection levels of Wave A to plot the most likely target zone for the termination of Wave C. We expect Wave C to end between the 100 percent and 127 percent projection of Wave A. You can see the annotated target zone that's noted in the illustration above.

Conservative approach

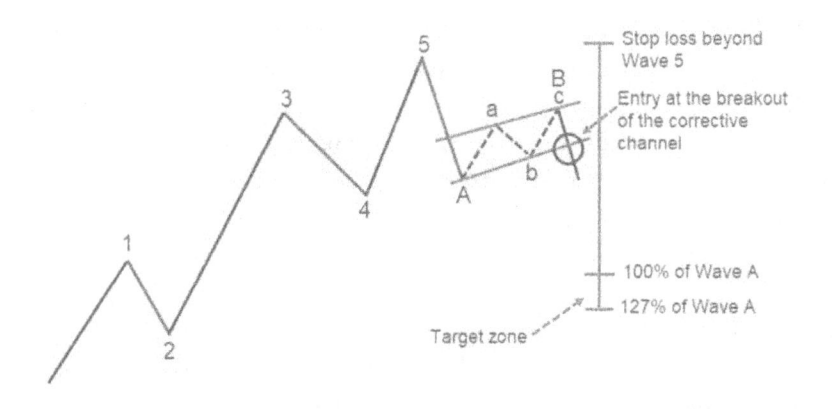

Figure 10-5: Conservative approach

Let's now talk about the conservative entries. Referring to this diagram, you can see the Wave B retracement which unfolds as a zigzag. We will draw a corrective channel around the zigzag structure by connecting the start of sub-wave a to the end of sub-wave b within the zigzag, and extending that line forward. Then, we would run a parallel of that line starting from the end of sub-wave a of the zigzag pattern. This would create the corrective channel as seen in this illustration. The **conservative option** generates the signal at the breakout of the corrective channel. This breakout is noted as shown by the circled area on this illustration. You'll notice that the conservative entry triggers quite a bit after the aggressive entry. Essentially, the second option requires more confirmation from the market than does the first option. As a result, we will tend to have a higher win rate while giving up some profit potential when using the second option.

The ***stop loss*** and the ***target zone*** for this option remain the same as in the aggressive approach.

In the next section, we'll go over the toolkit that we'll rely on for trading the Wave B retracement setup.

## Trade Toolkit

With Wave B, we should realize that it offers a low-risk opportunity to trade counter to the prevailing trend. The primary reason is that we have a very strong level that we're leaning against in this trade – the Wave 5 extreme. This major swing high within an uptrend represents a strong level of resistance, and the major swing low within a downtrend represents a strong level of support. Additionally, since this setup occurs near the end of the Elliott 5-3 cycle, it's easily recognizable on the price chart.

Traditional technical analysts will recognize the Wave B retracement setup as a head and shoulders pattern, with the end of Wave 3 representing the left shoulder, the end of Wave 5 representing the head, and the end of Wave B representing the right shoulder. However, unlike the traditional technical analyst who uses the head and shoulders pattern and relies on the break of the neckline to signal an entry, an Elliott Wave trader can enjoy better entries, especially in the case of an aggressive technique. The Elliott Wave approach allows for more granular analysis of the price action and offers a far greater edge.

So now, let's go over the toolkit that we'll need for trading the Wave B retracement setup as below:

- Fibonacci Projection: To measure the length of Wave 3;
- Awesome Oscillator: To confirm Divergence between Wave 3 and Wave 5;
- Self-confirmation: To confirm the end of Wave 5.
- Fibonacci Retracement: To plot the aggressive entry zone;
- Corrective Channel: To locate the conservative entry;
- Fibonacci Projection: To plot the target zone;

With all that background in mind, we'll move on to looking at some real chart examples for trading the Wave B retracement setup.

## Trade Example 1

Figure 10-6: Trade analysis

153

On this Pound Sterling/Swiss Franc daily chart, we can see Wave (1) kicks off the downtrend, followed by a fairly sharp retracement in Wave (2). Then, we have a strong price decrease as momentum starts to pick up in Wave (3). This is followed by a Wave (4) retracement, and finally, another price decrease in Wave (5). This marks the end of the impulse sequence and the corrective phase begins.

After the end of Wave (A) of the corrective phase, we see the price begin to decline and carve out a zigzag pattern within Wave (B). This pattern is labeled with the letters a-b-c as you can see on the chart. Soon afterward, the price begins to increase as the progress in Wave (C) starts to unfold.

Let's now see how we might have proceeded after recognizing this potential setup and review the different components of this trade setup. The first thing that we'll analyze is the presence of Wave (3) price action in the preceding impulse structure. We'll do this by first applying the Fibonacci projection tool and measuring the length of Wave (3) in relation to the length of Wave (1). In this case, Wave (3) easily extended beyond the minimum length requirement. Additionally, for this particular setup, we can see that Wave (5) exceeds the extreme of Wave (3). When this happens, we know that this is a typical Wave (5) price action, and can provide a higher probability trade setup.

Next, we'll perform another analysis in this price chart to see what self-confirmation for Wave (5) is telling us. To do this, we'll need to plot a trend line that connects the end of Wave (2) to the end of Wave 4 (keep in mind that we want to connect the ends, not the extremes of the two waves). After that trend line has been plotted, we will use it as a reference point to measure the time from the end of Wave (5) to the touch of the (2)-(4) trend line. In addition, we'll also measure the time that transpires for the completion of Wave (5). Then, we will compare these two from the time perspective to see whether self-confirmation for Wave (5) has occurred. Ultimately, we'll want the time from the end of Wave (5) to the touch of the (2)-(4) trend line to be less than or equal to the time for Wave (5) to complete. In this case, the time for the touch of the (2)-(4) trend line is clearly less than that for Wave (5) to complete. As such, we can say that self-confirmation for Wave (5) has occurred which fulfills the requirement for this filter.

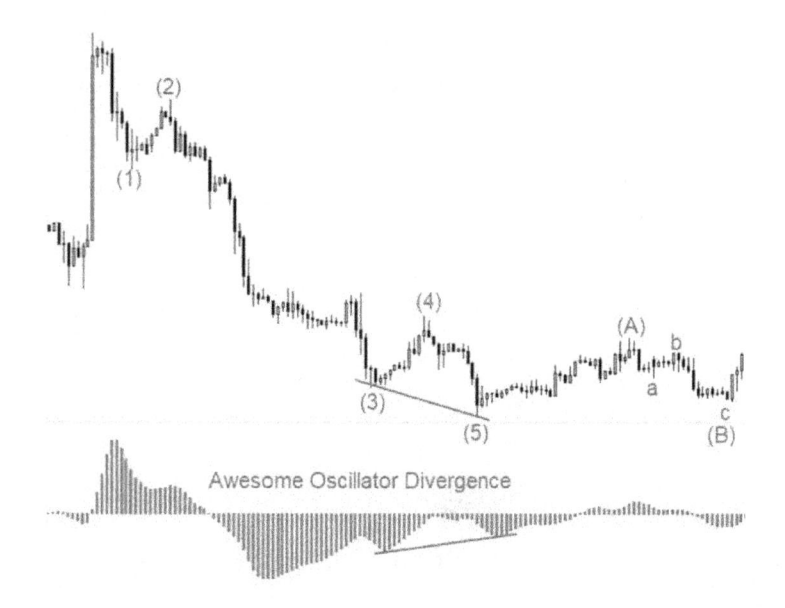

Figure 10-7: Trade analysis

In the following step, we will look to confirm a divergence pattern is present. In this picture, you can see that Wave (5) makes a lower low compared to Wave (3). Meanwhile, the awesome oscillator registers a higher low at Wave (5) compared to its peak at Wave (3). As such, a bullish divergence pattern can be confirmed between the price action and the awesome oscillator.

Now, with all those studies taken into account, we can confidently say that a high probability opportunity exists within this Wave (B) retracement setup. We'll look for a desirable location to enter into this trade in anticipation of catching the end of the Wave (B) retracement.

## Aggressive approach

Figure 10-8: Aggressive approach

Let's first apply the aggressive approach. The aggressive entry of this trade setup occurs when the price moves into the retracement zone that's created by the 50 percent and 62 percent retracement levels of Wave (A). As you can see, a buy limit order entry anywhere within that retracement zone would have been triggered. Regarding the stop-loss, we'll want to place that below the Wave (5) extreme as can be seen by the horizontal line at the bottom of this chart. The target zone is plotted using the 100 percent and 127 percent projection levels of Wave (A) measured from the termination point of Wave (B). You can see how the price moved into the target zone and resulted in a profitable exit anywhere within this area.

Conservative approach

Figure 10-9: Conservative approach

Let's move on to the conservative approach. On this chart view, you can see that the a-b-c zigzag within the corrective Wave (B) has been outlined using the corrective channel. We will first connect the start of sub-wave a with the end of sub-wave b. Then, we would take the parallel of that line and run it from the end of sub-wave a. Once the corrective channel is in place, we'll want to wait for a breakout and close above the corrective channel to signal the entry. In this example, the price moves higher after completing the zigzag pattern within Wave (B), ultimately breaking and closing beyond the higher boundary of the corrective channel. This is shown within the circled area on the price chart.

The stop loss would be placed below the extreme of Wave (5). Furthermore, for the potential take-profit area, we will the 100 percent and 127 percent Fibonacci projection of Wave (A) to fill that role.

Although this conservative approach may have a higher win rate than the aggressive technique, that will come at the cost of reducing your realized profit in relation to your potential loss on the trade. While this may not always be so pronounced, on a relative basis, the aggressive approach would generally provide a more favorable execution level.

## Trade Example 2

Figure 10-10: Trade analysis

On this Australian Dollar/Swiss Franc 4-hour chart, you can see the labeled impulse waves as they move in an uptrend. You can also see the labeled Waves (A) and (B) of the corrective phase that follows. Within Wave (B), you can see the a-b-c notations representing the three-wave upward move. This structure appears to be a typical zigzag pattern. Now, let's take a deeper dive into the overall structure and determine whether an ideal trading opportunity might exist.

Firstly, I've plotted the Fibonacci projection of Wave (1) to locate the minimum length of Wave (3). The lower line represents this minimum – the 150 percent projection level. The prices easily reach this level, and in fact, move far beyond it. Moreover, you can see that Wave (5) did exceed the Wave (3) swing high, satisfying the second requirement.

Next, we want to analyze the self-confirmation for Wave (5). We start by drawing a trend line that connects the ends of Wave (2) and Wave (4). You'll notice that we cannot effectively apply this filter in this particular case due to the very short price move within Wave (4). As you know, to verify self-confirmation for Wave (5), the time for the price to touch the (2)-(4) trend line starting from the end of Wave (5) must not be greater than the time for Wave (5) to form. Because of the angle that results from the (2)-(4) trend line, we are unable to practically apply this analysis in this example. This situation may occur from time to time, and when it does, you should not become confused about the implications. Instead, you would just go ahead and bypass this filter altogether for that particular setup because it doesn't provide any valuable information.

Figure 10-11: Trade analysis

Finally, we've included the awesome oscillator on this chart to confirm the divergence between the price action and the awesome oscillator. You can see that Wave (5) makes a higher high than Wave (3) on the price chart while the awesome oscillator registers a lower high during the same period. This creates a bearish divergence pattern between Waves (3)-(5) and the awesome oscillator.

This divergence pattern serves as additional evidence that supports the Wave (B) retracement setup.

So now, with that backdrop in mind, we would want to start monitoring the price action as Wave (A) completes in the expectation of a long position.

Aggressive approach

Figure 10-12: Aggressive approach

We know that the aggressive entry for this setup would occur as the price enters the 50 percent – 62 percent retracement zone of Wave (A). Notice we would have entered a sell limit order within that zone as sub-wave a within Wave (B) was forming. At that time, we would not have even labeled sub-wave a on the chart. Instead, we would have relied more on our knowledge of Fibonacci relationships between waves to execute the entry. As you can see from this chart, we would have enjoyed a favorable entry anywhere within the zone.

As part of the OCO order, we would place the stop loss beyond the extreme of Wave (5) as shown by the horizontal line. The target zone consists of the 100 percent and 127 percent Fibonacci projection of Wave (A). Notice on this setup, the price begins to move lower after completing sub-wave c within the Wave (B). The price moved into the target zone, however, it didn't reach the lower boundary of the zone. As I've mentioned several times by now, the most common relationship for Wave (C) is the one-to-one relationship with Wave (A), meaning that it will often travel and terminate upon reaching a distance equal to Wave (A).

## Conservative approach

Figure 10-13: Conservative approach

Let's see how we could have traded the setup using the conservative approach. We'll start off by plotting the corrective channel for the price action within Wave (B). Once the corrective channel is in place, we will wait for a breakout and close below this channel. The candle within the circled area shows where that breakout signal occurs. It appears to be a strong bearish marubozu candlestick, starting near the low and ending near the high. Once this candle completes, we would enter a short position using a market order for the entry. As we are well aware by now, the way that we would manage the exits is by placing a stop loss beyond the extreme of Wave (5) and a take-profit order within the target zone. Both the stop loss level and the target zone are noted on this chart. After the breakout to the downside, the price didn't have much difficulty entering the target zone.

Now that we've studied the mechanics of trading the Wave B retracement setup in quite some detail, you should be getting more comfortable with applying it on your own. Continuing forward, we will begin to learn an important trading setup occurring at the start of each Elliott Wave cycle.

# CHAPTER 11: TRADING STRATEGY NO.4

## Trade analysis

We've gone through quite a few strategies in this book and I hope you're beginning to piece everything together. In this chapter, we'll learn the fourth setup within my arsenal. This setup occurs at the end of the Wave C corrective phase.

Wave C ends the corrective phase and also completes an Elliott Wave cycle of one degree. Since the setup occurs at the end of a full cycle, I refer to it as the **Wave C completion setup**. We'll be diving more deeply into the mechanics of trading this setup shortly. But first, let's go over some forms of corrective phases within a complete Elliott Wave cycle.

Now that we know two common ways that the A-B-C corrective pattern can unfold are "zigzag" and "regular flat", we'll take a look at both of these variations within the corrective structure, starting with the zigzag correction.

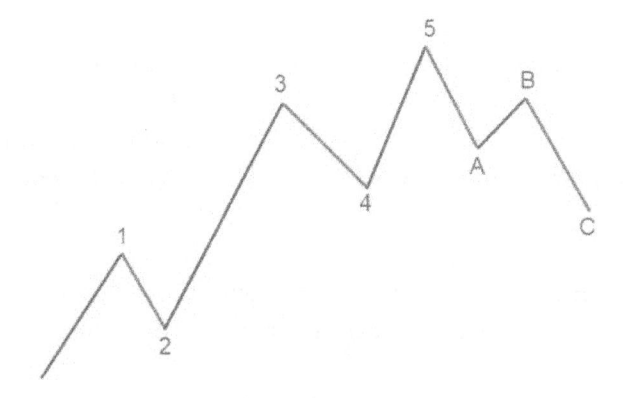

Figure 11-1: Corrective phase as a zigzag

You can see the illustration of the A-B-C corrective which unfolds as a simple zigzag. Typically, we will have a fairly sharp Wave A correction following the Wave 5 impulse. This will be followed by a Wave B retracement which will be less than the 79 percent retracement level of Wave A, typically at a 50 percent - 62 percent for the B leg within the zigzag. Moreover, the B leg within the zigzag itself will often be a zigzag pattern. Once Wave B completes, it will kick off Wave C of the corrective phase. The price will typically travel beyond the end of Wave A during the Wave C progression, and end at a distance that is often equal to the distance traveled in Wave A. Additionally, the time for Wave A to form is often equivalent to that of Wave C. Although this time relationship is not always as reliable as the one-to-one relationship in length, it is something that can be helpful in our analysis from time to time.

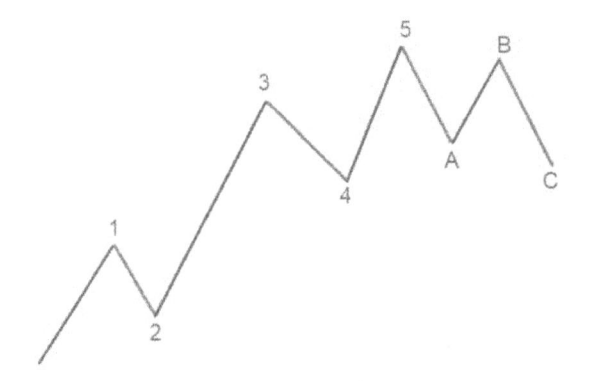

Figure 11-2: Corrective phase as a regular flat

Now, let's look at another common variation within the corrective phase. In this illustration, you can see that the corrective A-B-C structure unfolds as a regular flat. Remember that in a regular flat, Wave B will retrace Wave A by at least 80 percent. Additionally, Wave C will extend slightly beyond the end of Wave A.

As we move on to the next lecture, we'll begin to piece together the various trade management techniques that can be applied to this setup.

# Trade Execution

## Aggressive approach

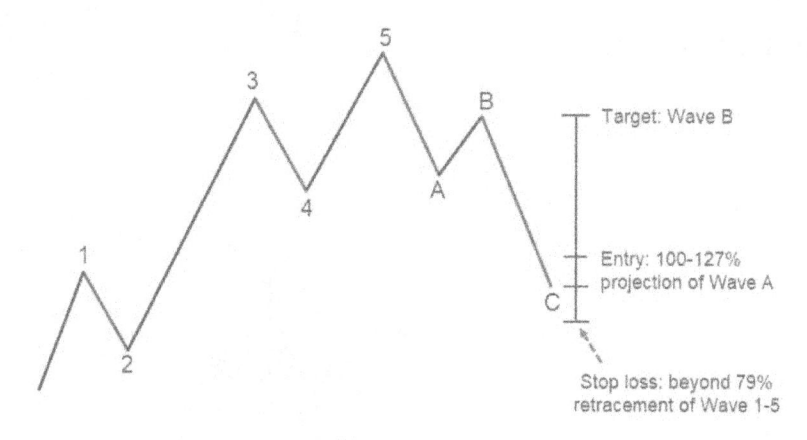

Figure 11-3: Aggressive approach

Let's go ahead and discuss some techniques that we will utilize to trade the Wave C completion setup. We'll start with the aggressive approach. As you may guess, the **aggressive entry** for the Wave C completion setup is triggered when the price enters the zone created by the 100 percent and 127 percent projection levels of Wave A as measured from the end of Wave B. We will typically want to use a limit order for the aggressive entry as the price is moving into the zone. I prefer to place the limit order entry closer to the 100 percent level as that level represents the higher probability termination point for Wave C. Depending on each specific situation, I may scale into the entry with a limit order to enter one-third of the position at the 100 percent level, a limit order to enter another third of the position at the midpoint of the zone, and the last order to enter the final third of the position at the 127 percent level.

Regarding the **stop loss** for this setup, we will use the 79 percent retracement level of the preceding impulse sequence of the same degree. More specifically, the stop loss will be placed beyond the 79 percent retracement of Waves (1) through (5) of the prior impulse. The **target** will be placed just before the swing extreme seen in Wave B. Essentially, for a long position, the swing high within Wave B will be used as the uppermost target for this setup. Conversely, for a short position, the swing low within Wave B will be used as the lowermost target for the setup. There will be some variations to this based on some other factors that we will be discussing when we are studying the actual setups on the price charts, but for now, it's important to understand these core placements.

Conservative approach

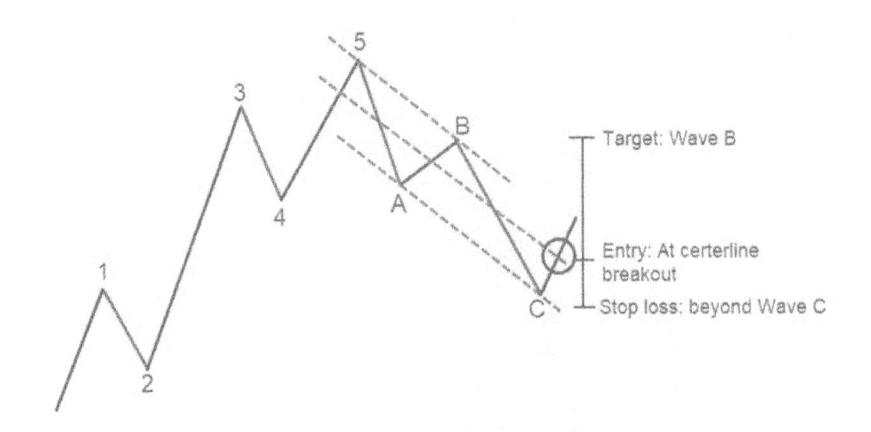

Figure 11-4: Conservative approach

Regarding the conservative approach for the Wave C completion setup, a variation of the channel technique can be used. We will draw a corrective channel and use the center line of the channel to trigger the **conservative entry**. To create the channel, we'll start with the Waves 5-B trendline - a trendline will connect the end of Wave 5 of the prior impulse to the end of Wave B. Then, a parallel line will be extended from the end of Wave A, completing the corrective channel. A center line will then be plotted within the corrective channel. Most charting platforms will allow you to plot a center line within a price channel. However, if your charting software doesn't have that feature, you can simply plot a parallel trendline and manually position it at the center of the channel.

Notice the circled area on this diagram which illustrates the **breakout point**. The breakout point occurs when the price **moves beyond** and **closes beyond** the center line of the corrective channel.

Moving on to the *stop-loss* placement, we will want to place that beyond the extreme of Wave C. Bear in mind that if the center line breakout is in fact Wave 1 of the new impulse sequence, the end of Wave C would also correlate to the beginning of Wave 1. As such, any retracement of Wave 1 must not exceed 100 percent retracement of Wave 1. This is an unbreakable Elliott Wave rule, and we can use that rule to place a logical stop loss for this setup. If, however, we find that the price moves beyond the Wave C extreme, that would invalidate our Wave 1 count following the termination of Wave C. In such a scenario, it's more likely that Wave C is still in progress. Can you see how knowing and understanding the different rules and guidelines within the Elliott Wave theory can help us in determining the most suitable areas to enter and exit the trades?

Finally, the *target area* will remain the same as with our previously mentioned aggressive approach.

Unlike many waves within the overall Elliott Wave cycle that have an intrinsic relationship to one or more other waves within the cycle, Wave 1 of an impulse doesn't really provide us with any reliable Fibonacci relationships with prior waves within the overall cycle. As such, the termination of Wave 1 following the end of Wave C is difficult to project. Therefore, we will need to use some other methods for taking profits during the Wave C completion setup. Having said that, I've found that within this setup, the Wave B high will often act as resistance in a long position and as support in a short position. The most logical target for the Wave C completion setup is, therefore, the swing extreme seen within Wave B. Sometimes, when Wave 1 turns out to be relatively short, the target will be reached during the Wave 3 progression. On the other hand, when Wave 1 turns out to be relatively long, the target will be reached very quickly.

In the following section, we'll discuss the toolkit that we'll rely on for effectively trading the Wave C completion setup.

## Trade Toolkit

Let's continue our discussion of the Wave C completion setup. As you should know by now, this setup coincides with a completed Elliott Wave cycle of one degree. Upon completion of this cycle, we will see the market resume in the direction of the larger degree trend. Since the setup occurs near the end of the 5-3 cycle, it's often quite easy to recognize on the price chart. As a result, we often have sufficient time to analyze the price action leading to this setup and be able to prepare for it. We can incorporate two different entry methods, in which the aggressive approach will allow us to enter into the position a bit earlier than the conservative approach. Both of these techniques will have their own risk profile. You can decide to use one or the other, or a combination of the two when initiating a new position.

Here are the different technical tools within our toolkit to trade the Wave C completion setup effectively.

- Corrective channel: To confirm the Wave C price action;
- Fibonacci Retracement: To validate the entry zone;
- Fibonacci Projection: To locate the aggressive entry zone;
- Corrective Channel: To determine the conservative entry;
- Fibonacci Retracement: To locate the stop loss placement;

Next, let's turn to some concrete chart examples that incorporate all of these different studies for the Wave C completion setup.

# Trade example 1

Figure 11-5: Trade analysis

Let's now turn our attention to the first trade example for the Wave (C) setup. You can see the five-wave impulse structure followed by the three-wave corrective sequence labeled (A), (B), and (C). This (A)-(B)-(C) correction appears to be a zigzag formation.

As the price was completing the 5-3 Elliott Wave cycle, we'll start by analyzing the price action through the corrective channel. On this chart, you can see the corrective channel has been plotted by connecting the extremes of Waves (5) and (B), and running a parallel line of that trend line off the end of Wave (A). We want the price action to be contained within the corrective channel. Specifically, since the goal of this corrective channel is to measure the price action for Wave (C), we want to ensure that Wave (C) does not extend far beyond the corrective channel. This condition is satisfied in this case although the two bars at the end of Wave (C) appear to move slightly outside of the corrective channel. There will be times when this occurs, especially during the termination point or turning point at the end of Wave (C). For that reason, I don't strictly require that the entire price action within Wave (C) remain within the corrective channel. Now, that may lead to some ambiguity about what exactly I mean by not extending far beyond the corrective channel? But don't worry, I do have an objective guideline below.

If an entire bar measured from high to low is outside the corrective channel, I would consider that as a movement that has moved beyond the corrective channel. This stricter definition is more objective, and for the most part, if you follow that guideline, you will be in adherence to this filter.

Next, I'd like to see the Wave (C) price movement to enter the 50 percent - 79 percent retracement of Waves 1-5 of the prior impulse. This retracement zone is a critical aspect of Wave (C) completion setup. Notice the dashed line connecting the start of Wave (1) and the end of Wave (5) in calculating these levels. Similar to the minimum requirement for Wave (3) that we discussed as part of some of our earlier strategies, the 50 percent retracement level acts as the minimum requirement for entering a new position within this setup.

We cannot always be confident whether the entire 5-3 structure is actually Waves (3) and (4) of a larger degree or something else within the overall cycle. When this is uncertain, there's a higher likelihood that the correction is occurring during some other stages within the overall cycle. Accordingly, I prefer to use the more prevalent 50 percent – 79 percent range of the prior impulse as the important entry zone filter. Also, we don't want the price to move beyond the 79 percent threshold. When this happens, it's likely that we have incorrectly labeled either the prior impulse or the A-B-C corrective, or both.

## Aggressive approach

Figure 11-6: Aggressive approach

Now that you've gained some background as to why I use the 50 percent - 79 percent retracement of the prior impulse as my entry zone filter, let's go straight to the strategy with Wave (C). The aggressive entry zone for the Wave (C) completion setup is created using the 100 percent and 127 percent projection of Wave (A) measured from the end of Wave (B). You'll remember that the outer lines on this chart represent the 50 percent and 79 percent retracement of the prior impulse. Hence, in this case, the aggressive entry zone is completely within the Wave 1-5 retracement zone. We can place a *buy limit order* anywhere within this area to open a position. The *stop loss* would be placed below the larger entry zone filter (the 79 percent level on the chart). Once the long entry is triggered, we would look to *take profits* just below the price extreme within Wave (B).

Notice that your buy limit order would have been executed at any point within the aggressive entry zone, and there was not much jeopardy of getting stopped out as prices began to move higher. The take profit level was triggered just below the Wave (B) extreme as can be seen on the upper end of this chart.

Conservative approach

Figure 11-7: Conservative approach

We'll now move on to discussing the conservative strategy for the Wave (C) completion setup. The conservative approach requires that the price break out and close beyond the center line of the corrective channel. Notice we've drawn the corrective channel, starting with the construction of the Waves 5-B trendline and then running a parallel line from the end of Wave (A). The center line is then plotted within this corrective channel. Notice the bar within the circled area that breaks above the center line of the corrective channel and manages to close above it. At the time of the breakout, the price has moved above the entry zone filter created by the 50 percent and 79 percent retracement levels of the prior impulse. This is completely acceptable and generally a good sign. As long as the price entered the minimum retracement zone prior to the breakout signal, it satisfies this requirement.

The stop loss for the conservative approach would be placed below the Wave (C) extreme. The take-profit target remains the same as with the aggressive approach. As you can see, the price hardly had any difficulty reaching the target.

Now, I hope you're beginning to understand how we can apply this setup in the real market charts. Let's move to the second example below.

# Trade example 2

Figure 11-8: Trade analysis

In this example, we are looking at the Australian Dollar/Japanese Yen 4-hour chart. After a five-wave impulse, we have a corrective phase in the (W)-(X)-(Y) formation. Don't let that confuse you since the implications for trading the (W)-(X)-(Y) correction will be the same as that of the (A)-(B)-(C) correction. Remember that a (W)-(X)-(Y) correction is simply a double combination or a double three as it's often referred to. In this case, we have a zigzag formation for Wave (W), and another zigzag formation in wave (Y), with the (X) wave being the connecting wave between these two zigzags. Hence, this structure is a double zigzag pattern.

Let's move on and make some quick assessment about this trade setup. First, we'll draw the corrective channel by creating the (5)-(X) trend line and running a parallel of that line through the end of wave (W). We want to make sure that the Wave (Y) price action doesn't extend completely beyond the channel. As you can see, near the termination point of the (Y) leg, there are some candles which penetrated below the lower line of the corrective channel. However, since a portion of those candles remained inside the channel, this would satisfy the requirement. Next on the agenda, we want to make sure that the price in the correction phase entered the 50 percent – 79 percent retracement zone, and at the same time, has not moved below the 79 percent retracement threshold. As you can see from this chart, this condition is also fully satisfied.

## Aggressive approach

Figure 11-9: Aggressive approach

Now it's time to plot the aggressive entry zone on this chart. Using the Fibonacci projection tool, we'll project the length of Wave (W) off the end of Wave (X). The levels of interest will be the 100 percent and 127 percent projection levels, which is the entry zone. Notice how some candles just touches the upper boundary of this entry area before prices start to move higher. The stop loss would be placed below the 79 percent retracement level. Moreover, our take-profit price would easily be reached once placed around the top of Wave (X).

Conservative approach

Figure 11-10: Conservative approach

Let's come to the conservative approach. On this chart, you can see the center line of the corrective channel plotted as well. The entry signal would occur when the price breaks and closes above the center line of this corrective channel. The strong breakout bar within the circled area confirms the conservative entry signal. Notice it's a strong bullish candle that resembles a marubozu candlestick pattern. Once the long position was initiated, we would have seen the price fall back lower twice to test the center line of the channel. After the second re-test, the price began its sharp move to the upside, touching the target level. The stop loss would be placed below the extreme of the (Y) leg. The target would remain the same as with the aggressive approach - the Wave (X) swing high.

With that, we'll conclude the chapter on the Wave C completion setup. In the next chapter, we'll discuss the final setup within my trading arsenal – the one that every Elliott Wave trader wouldn't want to miss.

# CHAPTER 12: TRADING STRATEGY NO.5

### Trade analysis

Up to now, we've discussed four different setups within the Elliott Wave framework: **Wave 4 retracement setup**, **Wave 5 diagonal setup**, **Wave B retracement setup**, and **Wave C completion setup**. In this chapter, I'll share with you the fifth and final high probability setup within my trading arsenal. This setup occurs after one complete Elliott Wave cycle. It looks to take advantage of Wave 3 during a new impulse sequence. I refer to this setup as **Wave 3 continuation setup**.

We've known that after Wave C of the corrective phase completes, the entire cycle will repeat itself. As it does, we can try to capture one of the most elusive yet profitable legs within the entire Elliott Wave cycle - Wave 3. Wave 3 is considered a wonder to behold. If we were able to get on board the Wave 3 move early enough, this would allow us to generate an outsized amount of gains relative to other waves within the overall cycle.

Following the end of Wave C in an overall bull market, I look for Wave 1 to kick off the new impulse phase, and then wait for the pullback in Wave 2 or a breakout above the Wave 1 extreme to ride Wave 3. The same goes for an overall bear market but in reverse. We'll go over the exact entry details for trading the Wave 3 continuation setup a bit later, but for now, it's important that you understand where this setup occurs within the overall Elliott Wave cycle.

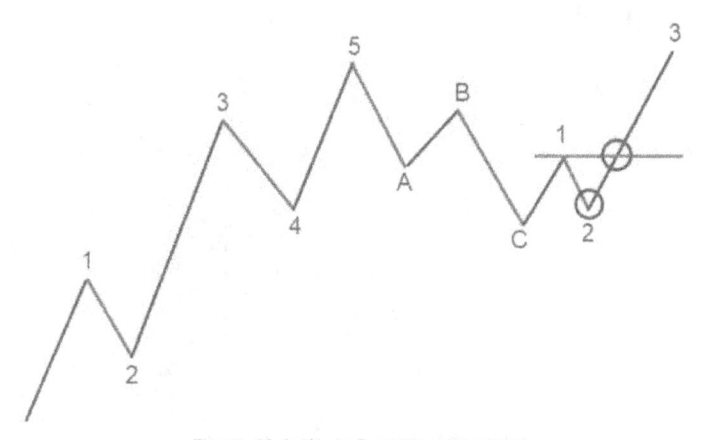

Figure 12-1: Wave 3 continuation setup

This illustration shows a complete 5-3 cycle, including 5 waves of the impulse and 3 waves of the corrective. In addition to that, it also displays the continuation of the bullish trend after the A-B-C corrective phase. The two circled areas on this chart represent the two significant areas that we can try to take advantage of in riding the price action within Wave 3. Since Wave 3 is typically the longest wave within the entire Elliott Wave cycle, it's highly advisable to narrow in on it during its early progression. Sometimes, that's easier said than done because the overall structure that houses this setup can be difficult to recognize in real-time market conditions. Nevertheless, due to the highly profitable nature of trading Wave 3, it's well worth the effort.

# Trade Execution

## Aggressive approach

Figure 12-2: Aggressive approach

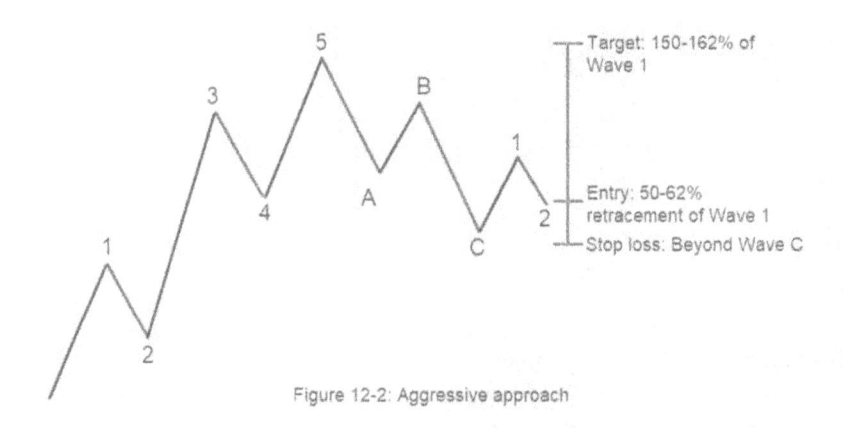

The optimal entry techniques for Wave 3 continuation setup entail understanding where the most likely terminations of Wave 2 will be. As you may recall from the earlier chapters, Wave 2 tends to be a fairly deep retracement. In a large percentage of cases, we would expect Wave 2 to retrace Wave 1 between 50 percent and 62 percent levels. Based on the statistical significance of this zone, I will use this area as the ***aggressive entry*** for the Wave 3 continuation setup. If I find that Wave 1 is relatively long and displays an impulsive behavior, I will skew my limit order entry closer to the 50 percent retracement level. If, however, I find that Wave 1 is just fairly sized or is relatively small, I opt to skew my limit order entry closer to the 62 percent retracement level. Having said that, in many cases, I would simply place a limit entry order around the midpoint of these two levels.

Again, as I've touched on several times in this book, there are many ways that you can incorporate the aggressive approach into your trading. There's ***no magical way*** that works all the time. You'll need to analyze the price action and your overall bias, and then decide where you want to place the entry order within the high probability reversal zone.

Now, as far as the stop loss goes, it should be placed beyond the end of Wave C which is also the start of Wave 1 of the new cycle. As you already know, one of the unbreakable rules within Elliott Wave is that Wave 2 can never retrace more than 100 percent of Wave 1. If it does, our overall count needs to be re-evaluated because our original assumption is incorrect somewhere. This is very valuable information that we can use in incorporating the *stop loss* level for this setup. Next, let's discuss the potential profit side of this trade. If you've been paying attention up till now, you should know that Wave 3 is often a 162 percent projection of Wave 1 as measured from the end of Wave 2. You can see in this illustration that I've used the 150 percent and the 162 percent levels of Wave 1 to compose the *target zone* for the setup. It should be noted that although Wave 3 often travels 162 percent the length of Wave 1, we'll want to take our profits before the termination of Wave 3. I'm not looking to pick the exact top of Wave 3 in an uptrend, nor am I looking to pick the exact bottom of Wave 3 in a downtrend. If I can get the bulk of the move and still exit before the most probable turning point, then I will be more than happy. As a result, I will often choose to exit my position at either the 150 percent level or the midpoint of the 150 percent and 162 percent levels.

Conservative approach

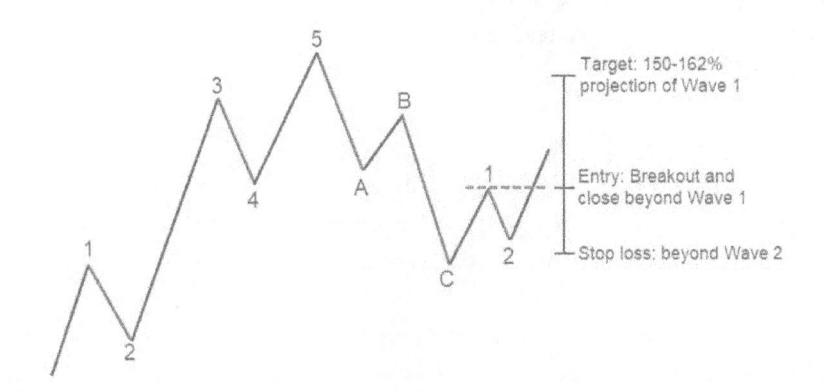

Figure 12-3: Conservative approach

Let's move on to discussing the conservative approach for the Wave 3 continuation setup. With this method, we'll require more confirmation from the market that Wave 3 is in fact in progress. In this illustration, notice Wave

1-2 following the A-B-C correction. Once Wave 2 correction ends and we can recognize the very early stages of a possible wave, we will draw a horizontal resistance line off the swing high of Wave 1 (the dashed line). The **conservative entry** will come as the price breaks out and closes beyond the end of Wave 1.

The **stop loss** for the conservative strategy would be placed beyond the Wave 2 extreme, which is below the Wave 2 swing low in this case. As for the **target zone**, it remains the same as in the aggressive approach.

Now, you should have a fairly good idea of what constitutes a potential Wave 3 continuation setup. We'll be looking at some real charts shortly so that you can get even more comfortable with the technique. But before we do that, let's go over the necessary trade toolkit for this setup.

## Trade Toolkit

Though Wave 3 is often the most powerful and potentially most profitable way to trade, it is quite difficult at times to correctly label. In many times, what we believe to be the early stages of a Wave 3 move may turn out to be Wave C instead. As a result, it's important that we are careful and objective in the wave labeling to ensure that we realize the highest chances of capturing a real Wave 3 price move.

One of the best signs of the Wave 3 leg is the momentum that accompanies the price action within it. Specifically, the price incline is very sharp in a Wave 3 impulse. We'll often see a momentum peak register at the end of Wave 3 within the awesome oscillator as well as other momentum-based indicators.

One thing that's very important when trading the Wave 3 leg is to practice patience once the price begins to move in the intended direction. If we time the Wave 3 continuation setup properly, we can often enjoy a risk-to-reward ratio of 1:3 or more, especially if we use an aggressive entry for the trade. We have to be patient and let the trade play out and not be tempted to exit prematurely. Jesse Livermore, one of the greatest traders once said: *it was never my thinking that made me big money, it was always my sitting that made me big money.* That's exactly the mindset that we need to apply when we're trading the Wave 3 continuation setup. Here is where using the simple set-and-forget trade management technique shines. Once you're in the trade, place the hard stop and take-profit targets, and then just walk away and let the trade just play out.

Below are some tools that we'll rely on for trading the Wave 3 continuation setup.

- Fibonacci Retracement: To analyze the prior correction;
- Corrective Channel: To confirm Wave 1 price action;
- Self-Confirmation: To confirm the end of Wave C;
- Fibonacci Retracement: To plot the aggressive entry zone;
- Fibonacci Projection: To plot the target zone;

With all information in mind, I believe we're now ready to explore the best chart examples in the Wave 3 continuation setup in the next sections.

## Trade Example 1

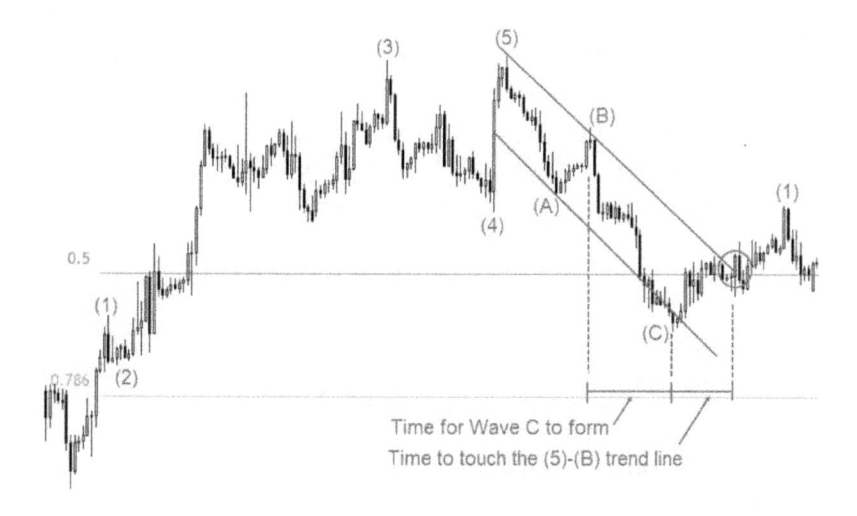

Figure 12-4: Trade analysis

Let's turn our attention to this 2-hour price chart of the Euro/Pound Sterling pair. We can see the impulse Waves (1) through (5) and the (A)-(B)-(C) correction labeled. From there, we've gone on to label Wave (1) within the new impulse phase.

After the formation of the Waves (1) that follow the previous cycle, we can go ahead and plot the 50 percent - 79 percent retracement zone of the prior impulse. Essentially, with this filter, we want the (A)-(B)-(C) correction to terminate within this zone. As we can see in this example, Wave (C) does terminate at the middle of the zone, so we can say that this initial requirement has been met.

Still on this chart, we want to confirm the new Wave (1) price action by drawing a corrective channel and wait for Wave (1) breaks out and closes beyond the (5)-(B) trend line of the corrective channel. You can see how the condition is satisfied with the circled area. Therefore, we can say that the wave labeling for the new Wave (1) impulse is most likely correct. Remember when drawing the corrective channel, you would plot a trend line that connects the end of Wave (5) to the end of Wave (B) (the (5)-(B) trend line). Then, you'll take a parallel of that trendline and extend it through the end of Wave (A). These two lines create the corrective channel.

After drawing the channel, we will assess the Wave (C) price action using the self-confirmation concept. In this case, we want to confirm that Wave (C) has been completed by assessing the time element for the Wave (C) progression to the touch of the (5)-(B) trend line. Specifically, the time to touch the (5)-(B) trendline should be less than or equal to the time for Wave (C) to form. In this example, our self-confirmation has passed the test.

## Aggressive approach

Figure 12-5: Aggressive approach

Now, with all these criteria met, we can start making preparations for a possible long position in this market. The aggressive entry for the Wave (3) continuation setup calls for a limit order entry within the 50 percent - 62 percent retracement zone of Wave (1). If you look closely, you can see as the price moved lower in Wave (2), it slightly penetrated the 62 percent level before quickly reversing to the upside. Hence, a buy limit order within the zone could have been triggered. The stop loss is placed just below the Wave (C) extreme which is also the start of Wave (1). The target zone is created using the 150 percent and 162 percent projection levels of Wave (1) as measured from the end of Wave (2). As you can see at the top right of the chart, our target zone was reached easily.

## Conservative approach

Figure 12-6: Conservative approach

Let's now shift to the conservative approach. If you recall, the conservative entry for the Wave (3) continuation setup calls for a breakout and close beyond the end of Wave (1). I've plotted the horizontal line (the higher one) which will serve as a signal line. Notice in the circled area that a candle breaks and closes above this level, confirming the breakout and triggering the conservative entry. A market buy order would be placed following this breakout bar.

Immediately following the conservative entry trigger, we can see there was some minor consolidation before the price moved higher to the designated target zone. Even though there was that minor consolidation after the entry, the trade was never in any real jeopardy of getting stopped out. Notice the stop loss is placed below the end of Wave (2) as shown on the chart while the target zone remains the same as in the aggressive approach.

# Trade example 2

*Figure 12-7: Trade analysis*

Let's look at one more example of the Wave (3) continuation setup. Notice the impulse phase of this downtrend which is labeled (1) through (5), and the corrective phase which moves upward and is labeled (W)-(X)-(Y). I've opted to label this corrective structure as a (W)-(X)-(Y) rather than an (A)-(B)-(C) because Waves (W) and (Y) appear to carve out three smaller waves, indicating that it is a double combination structure. In any case, whether this was labeled as an (A)-(B)-(C) or (W)-(X)-(Y) structure, the implication would remain the same. Keep in mind that with a (W)-(X)-(Y) pattern, it could extend further to form a (W)-(X)-(Y)-(X)-(Z) structure as well. If you're still a bit unclear about double and triple three combinations, it is highly recommended that you review the previous chapters on this topic so that you can become more comfortable labeling these types of corrections.

Now, let's take a look at how we would want to analyze the entire picture to see whether a viable trading opportunity exists. After the new Wave (1) completes, we would then look to plot the 50 percent - 79 percent retracement zone of the prior impulse. As per this filter, we want to see the corrective phase terminate within the plotted zone. In this particular example, the correction ended right in the middle of the retracement zone, thus fulfilling the first requirement for this trade setup.

Moving forward to the next step in the process, we draw a corrective channel to help confirm Wave (1) price action. The corrective channel is drawn, starting with the trend line that connects the end of Wave (5) and Wave (X). A parallel line of this trend line is then projected from the end of Wave (W). Notice the breakout shown within the circled area. The price action breaks below the (5)-(X) trend line and closes below it. Hence, the second key element for this trade setup has been verified.

We now need to turn to the self-confirmation filter to further bolster the viability of a potential short position. Once again, we refer to the (5)-(X) trend line for the time comparison purposes. In this example, it's evident that the self-confirmation for Wave (Y) has been met where the time for the price to touch the (5)-(X) trend line is less than the time for Wave (Y) to form. With this backdrop in mind, we can now turn our attention to trade execution.

<u>Aggressive approach</u>

Figure 12-8: Aggressive approach

Let's first take a look at the aggressive approach. The aggressive entry zone would be plotted using the 50 percent and 62 percent retracement levels of Wave (1). In this case, the retracement ends at the 50% retracement level before a strong decline appears. The stop loss level would be placed beyond the end of Wave (Y) which is also the start of Wave (1). The target zone is comprised of the 150 percent and 162 percent projection levels of Wave (1) measured from the end of Wave (2). You can see the target zone marked near the lower end of this chart. There were some back-and-forth price moves on the way to this designated zone, but eventually, the price started its descent and strongly crossed the target level.

Conservative approach

Figure 12-9: Conservative approach

Here's what the conservative strategy would have looked like. The conservative entry calls for a breakout and a close below the end of Wave (1). That level is represented by the circled area. There were some efforts made by the buyers after the breakout. However, with the stop loss placed above the Wave 2 extreme, the trade isn't put in any jeopardy during the course of execution. Moreover, the target zone remains the same as with the aggressive approach, providing a decent risk-to-reward ratio even when we opt for a conservative method.

Until now, we've gone over each of the five setups that I use within my overall trading plan. I know there's tons of information so far, and it's not easy to remember them right away. Therefore, it's highly recommended that you practice each strategy multiple times so that you can become more proficient in applying them in real-time market conditions. The more you practice with wave counts and wave analysis, the more confident you'll become in trading with Elliott Wave setups, which in turn will enable you to make consistent profits in the markets.

# CONCLUSION

I hope you've become enthusiastic about applying what you've learned so far in your practical trading. The five strategies that I've presented so far are high probability setups that took me years to test and systemize into an effective model. As far as I am concerned, incorporating Elliott Wave and Fibonacci tools is probably the best combination one can ever make in financial trading. They supplement each other in helping us to analyze, detect, execute, and optimize trade opportunities in the markets. The value they've brought to traders is timeless.

You've seen I use many filters in each strategy. The paramount purpose of incorporating so many barriers for our trades is to save you from arbitrary trading. Any experienced traders would agree with me that we are all susceptible to being distracted by the temptation of adding more trades. Arbitrary trading is one of the shortest ways of blowing up your account. With filters coming into play, I want to emphasize the *"quality over quantity"* principle. You might have heard about this principle in many other areas by different people, and in trading, it's of supreme importance. If you fail to stick to high-quality trades, you are planning to fail in the long term.

To grasp the best opportunity in the markets, the method alone is surely not enough. You also need a good mindset and paramount discipline. It might seem a bit vague on the surface, but in fact, it's not. One of the easiest and most effective ways in maintaining an appropriate mindset and managing trades is by using a trading plan. You can easily obtain a good trading plan for just a few bucks, or you can make one by yourself if you want. Just write down everything you need for effective trade execution as detailed as possible, then strictly follow them consistently, and see the magic happens. Remember, **understanding** and **being able to apply consistently** what you've learned are two different things.

Finally, every great thing takes time, and success in trading is not an exception. As I've mentioned a few times in this book, after a lot of practice, you'll be more familiar with the strategies, pattern recognition, filters, and more. The more you are familiar with these strategies and the more discipline you can cultivate over time, the closer you are to success. What do think is the thing that all losers have in common? If your answer is "give up", I would agree with you. Let's do the opposite: Practice with perseverance and a strong belief.

This brings us to the end of the book. I want to congratulate you on finishing this book, and strongly believe that you've made the right decision in taking your trading knowledge and skills to the next level. Now is the time to take action.

Last but not least, if you find you've received something useful in this book, kindly spend a few seconds leaving **an honest review** as a way to help other traders find a way to success.

# REFERENCES

Basics of Elliott Wave. Elearnmarkets.
https://www.elearnmarkets.com/school/units/basics-of-elliott-wave

Elliott Wave Theory: Rules, Guidelines and Basic Structures. Elliottwaveforecast.
https://elliottwave-forecast.com/elliott-wave-theory/

Chen, J. (2022, May 25). Impulse Wave Pattern. Investopedia.
https://www.investopedia.com/terms/i/impulsewave.asp

(2021, July 17). Impulse Wave Pattern – Rules and Fibonacci Calculations. Sweeglu.
https://sweeglu.com/impulse-wave-pattern/

(2017, September 22). How to Recognize a Leading Diagonal Pattern. Ewminteractive.
https://ewminteractive.com/recognize-leading-diagonal-pattern

(2014, April 05). Ending Diagonal? What is this? Ewminteractive.
https://ewminteractive.com/ending-diagonal-what-is-this

(2014, May 20). Truncated fifth wave. "The Black Swan". Ewminteractive.
https://ewminteractive.com/truncated-fifth-wave-the-black-swan

(2014, June 06). Expanding Flat and how to avoid its traps. Ewminteractive.
https://ewminteractive.com/expanding-flat-and-how-to-avoid-its-traps

(2016, May 18). The Mischievous Running Flat Correction. Ewminteractive.
https://ewminteractive.com/mischievous-running-flat-correction

Gorbatenko, E. What is a triangle? FBS
https://fbs.com/analytics/guidebooks/what-is-a-triangle-273#:~:text=What%20is%20a%20triangle%3F&text=Triangles%20are%20a%20correction%20five,wave%20B%20in%20a%20zigzag.

(2015, January 03). How To Read A Corrective Combination. Ewminteractive.
https://ewminteractive.com/how-to-read-a-corrective-combination

(2020, January 20). Elliott wave personality according to Prechter. Psychology of five-wave pattern. Litefinance. https://www.litefinance.com/blog/for-professionals/market-wave-theory-by-robert-prechter-part-2-psychology-of-five-wave-pattern/